COFFEE, CASTANETS AND DON QUIXOTE

The Unique Delights of Four Great Cities of Spain

by

Robert Noble Graham

Copyright 2013 Robert Noble Graham

1

By the Same Author

Novels

- Masks of Venice
- The Women from Crete
- The Celebrity of Anders Hecht

Travel

- Coffee in Cuba

About the Author

Robert Noble Graham had careers in the publishing, oil and financial services industry. He sold the business of which he was owner and Managing Director in 2009. He has had drama produced by BBC Radio 4 as well as local events in Scotland. He is the author of three published novels and one previous travel book. He speaks six languages and is a member of MENSA. His travel books are very much personal and often humorous accounts, informed by a wide knowledge of the history and culture. The novels also draw on his knowledge of and interest in European countries.

He is divorced with two adult children and lives in Scotland. He is interested in travel, languages, food and sport as well as being something of an authority on where the best coffee can be found almost anywhere in Europe.

SPAIN

Prologue

I hope this book brings the warmth, the variety,
the colour and the mystery of Spain at least in part.
It would be nice to think it's the best you can do
without actually finding your passport, fiddling
with internet sites and standing in hot queues at
the airport. It's not a travelogue or in any sense a
comprehensive guide to this magical country.
However, I hope I have captured some of the
drama, the excitement, the exoticism as well as the
pleasure of an idle lunch in the sunshine by the
Guadalquivir.

It describes visits I've made to four of its
wonderful cities. Each has a very distinct
personality and each showed sides of Spain that
are attractive, strange or comical. For some people
all that matters about the country are the beaches,
the sunshine and the wine. The Press tell us
something about the economic and social problems
that are besetting it along with the rest of southern
Europe. The real Spain goes on, as intricate as a
carpet from Isfahan with as many threads.

We are told that travel broadens the mind. It
certainly can do, but the mind has got to be open
to that possibility. For some people it simply
confirms their prejudices and for them they might
as well have stayed at home. If you are open to
new experiences then the reactions prompted by
the many faces of Spain can tell you some
surprising things about yourself as well as about

4

the fascinating life and history of a unique country.

I have travelled elsewhere in Spain and hope to write about that in due course. At this point I have visited marvellous sites like Granada, Ronda and some of the mountain villages around Altea. I have been to the Balearic and Canary Islands. I have not yet visited Cadiz, Salamanca or Zaragoza. I had no wish to write an interminable book about every backstreet I could find in Iberia. I wanted the book to be digestible, readable on an aeroplane flight or at times when, like exquisite wine or tapas, a taste to delight the senses is preferable to a three hour meal. For that reason I have confined myself to four cities, each of which made a huge impact on me.

Writing about Spain has intensified the awareness I had that here, perhaps more than most places, you cannot separate the past and the present. I become more certain with passing years that that is not possible anywhere. It is an illusion that the past is gone. What I write about these cities will show how keenly I was aware of this in Spain.

For readers in the New World who are kind enough to read my books and send me encouraging messages this book may serve a purpose I had not thought of until recently. Shortly before writing this prologue I spent some time in the state of Georgia in the United States. I was talking to a young man who had done a little travelling and intended to do much more. He made the point that nothing had prepared him for how different a European city is from a North American one. The availability of space is one reason for that of course, but also the fact that European cities usually began as compact communities that could be easily defended. They were also built in grossly non-egalitarian societies where the wealth and power of the King or the Church could commandeer what was effectively slave labour to create majestic buildings that would have been unaffordable in any modern economy. It is also true, however, that these cities have been transformed by the interest and spending power of the New World. Restaurants, hotels, bars and visitor centres abound now in Europe to a great extent because of the interest and spending power of visitors from across the Atlantic and from the Antipodes. Anyone who doubts this should read the remarkable book, "The Bible in Spain", recounting the adventures of the courageous and astonishingly multilingual George Borrow as he went from one flea-bitten, bedbug ridden hostelry to another to promote the Word in early 19th century Spain. I often wonder if Parisians who, in my experience, can be unfortunately anti-American, ever ponder how much they owe to Hollywood, American songwriters and Ernest Hemingway for the tremendous promotion their city has received from the US.

I have quite often found my own appreciation for a country is deepened by also seeing it through the eyes of another traveller, one who perhaps differs from me in age, taste and temperament. It would be nice to think I might achieve that to some degree with this small volume.

So, I hope you enjoy reading about my travels in Spain

6

BARCELONA

Barcelona was founded by the interestingly named William the Hairy about 1,000 years ago. He was one of the many Vikings who risked life, limb and anything else of importance in their haste to get out of Denmark or Norway in the Middle Ages. This was allegedly because there wasn`t much useful land in these countries and the first son got the whole farm so off went all the others. At least he didn`t feel he had to go as far as Turkey (the Varangian Guard were all Vikings), Russia (the Rus were a Viking tribe) or, remarkably, Canada. Given that most illustrations show Vikings as a mass of hair with eyes and swords popping out one wonders how shaggy William must have been to be identified as `hairy`. Given the notable talent for irony shown in Norse sagas it`s quite likely he was bald as a coot.

Whatever William`s motivations for settling in north easst Spain I`m sure mine for visiting were quite different. For various reasons I had begun to find Iberia a particularly interesting area. Its comparative geographic isolation, being bounded by water and the Pyrenees, its political isolation under Franco and its rich addition of Islamic influence for several centuries produced a country which has a very particular identity that many artists and many humble tourists have found fascinating. Barcelona, as the country`s second city in terms of population, clearly demanded a visit. I had no intention of booking dinner at the renowned best restaurant in the world, El Bulli, but I already knew enough of Spain to know that the chances of getting excellent food at reasonable

7

cost were very high. The region of which it is the capital, Catalonia, was also special for the number of gifted but extremely odd artists it has spawned. I was well aware of Salvador Dalí, Antoni Gaudí and Joan Miró and wondered if the key to their oddity would be apparent. For the benefit of anyone whose need to know the answer to that question is particularly urgent the outcome is disappointing. I left as ignorant as I arrived.

As well as fame for its artists and importance as a trading centre, Barcelona has another, less inviting reputation. For much of its history it has been known as one of the best places in Europe if you would want to be mugged. The guidebooks I read either skirted this aspect or discussed it as if it was entirely a historic problem that the authorities had effectively dealt with. I was to have a prime and memorable experience to illustrate that it is alive and active. I might have said `alive and well` but since I reckoned I had encountered the worst mugger in Europe it could perhaps better be described as `alive but ailing`. On the other hand, the city had in 1992 staged a very well managed Olympic Games which, I think, greatly enhanced its image as a modern and effective city.

I had booked a small hotel in the Calle Tallers just south of Plaça Catalunya since it was just beside Las Ramblas, the most famous street in the city and one of the few features I knew of. Ramblas is a very broad avenue with a central pavement between the traffic lanes. That central pavement is normally packed with stalls selling magazines, balloons, confectionery, pet mice, hyperactive budgies and guide books. At frequent intervals you will see `living statues`, presumably resting or unemployed actors or dancers dressed and painted to look like metal or stone. They have an impressive ability to remain motionless for long periods. Some spring into life or give the faintest wink when money is thrown in their box. I have watched some of them for long periods, usually from the comfort of a café and have never seen one sneeze, scratch an unbearable itch or run off to answer a call of nature. Even if I had the talents to practise such an art I think my basic distrust of animals and small children would deter me. However, I would imagine that Ramblas is a prime site and the temporary discomfort is probably well rewarded.

I was enjoying the sights of Ramblas on my first morning when my attention was captured by an opening on the south side of the street. It led to the renowned Boqueria market. Markets have been held on this site since around 1200 A.D. but the construction of an enclosed and covered area was agreed in the nineteenth century and completed in 1914. For anyone interested in food, especially fresh food, this is one of the unmissable sights of the city. Other cities have great buildings, artists, history etc but I don`t know of another with a market as extraordinary as this one. The range of fruit, vegetables, cheeses and spices is wonderful, but to me the most captivating display was the seafood. My home country is quite conservative about which products of the oceans it will eat. Spaniards do not seem to share this hesitation. Around me in La Boqueria I saw vendors in the middle of circular stalls which displayed an abundance of sea life, much of it still alive, twitching and planning escape. A langoustine was making an impressive if rather slow run for it across the tender bodies of other captives. Others, like barnacles, were not so tender. I was surprised to see them. I once tried to scrape a barnacle from a rock on the island of Barra and found it very hard work. I know that the islanders in the Hebrides would harvest barnacles when nothing else was on offer but I`m not sure they`d have bothered if the rest of La Boqueria had surrounded them. I find it difficult to believe the nutrition from a barnacle could ever replace the energy spent harvesting it, let alone cleaning and cooking it. The langoustine continued to pick his careful, determined way down the stall, bravely passing a fish which seemed to be all mouth with a tiny body attached as an afterthought. It looked depressed but I felt this might not simply be homesickness as it lay on the slab. It was easy to imagine he was a reincarnated glutton, punished in some Hindu universe by giving him a mouth large enough to seize huge portions but only the body to digest tiny ones. A couple of small octopi waved despairing arms as if hoping for attention from the stall owner, no doubt hoping to explain that there had been a ghastly mistake and they would be much more satisfying meals in a year`s time if allowed to swim the oceans a little longer.

One of my major aims was to see the Picasso Museum, permanently sited in the Barrio Gótico. Picasso was from Malaga originally but his father, also a gifted painter, got a job in Barcelona when Pablo was 12. The Barrio Gótico sits to the north of Ramblas and can be entered from it by one or other narrow alley. The name in Catalan simply means Gothic district. This may be because the cathedral is in gothic style but it may also reflect the fact that Wilfred the Hairy and his friends were not the only Germanic tribe to settle in the peninsula. The Goths who were among the tribes who sacked Rome in 420 A.D. and who probably originated from somewhere around modern Hungary obviously had a taste for warmer climes and many of them reached Spain. Whilst on that subject, Andalusia, the magical area in southern Spain, is so called because it was largely colonised by another Germanic tribe, the Wendels or Vandals, whose unruly behaviour gives us the modern word `vandal`. The locals had difficulty with an initial `w` sound as modern Spaniards still do so they dropped it, thus Andalusia instead of Wandalusia. Many of these Germanic tribes began to move because they in turn were displaced by Siberian tribes such as the Huns under Attila. Anyone such as Catalan nationalists or their counterparts in my own country of Scotland who believe there is some such racial entity as a Catalan or a Scot should learn some European history and understand that we in Europe are all twisted bundles of racial background.

The Barrio Gótico is the one part of the city which, in my view, has real atmosphere. It speaks of history, deeds and misdeeds, especially if you are brave enough to wander into it in the evening. The Picasso Museum resulted from a gift to the city by Picasso`s friend and secretary, Jaume Sabartes, and had the good fortune to be housed in the mediaeval courtyard palaces of Calle Moncada. Even if the contents were not so special the building would be well worth a visit for its own

11

charms. I've never been very sure what a Spanish *hidalgo* is or was but striding around the spacious rooms of the Picasso Museum makes me feel like one nonetheless. Having the tastes that I do, my interest in these museums is not wholly cultural and lofty. Without exception in my experience Spanish museums have some of the best cafés in Europe. Given that I find wandering around museums infinitely more tiring than a workout in the gym this facility is of great importance. The Picasso Museum shows work of the young artist from age 12 onwards. It appears that even from adolescence he had no trouble drawing or painting anything that took his fancy. This gave me a different perspective on his later phases. If you could paint like Rubens or Goya at the age of twelve what would you do with the rest of your life? Answer? Seduce a lot of women and invent cubism. Looking at his later work in the Prado or Thyssen- Bornemisza in Madrid the triangular women in bright yellow become more understandable. The fact that they are usually in floods of tears (not surprising if you have unexpectedly become triangular) does not detract from the terrific vitality so many of them exhibit. If you want to learn to appreciate Picassso visit one of the Spanish galleries such as the Prado in Madrid and spend some time with the gloomy crucifixions and self-immolations of Ribera and Zurbaran, worthy chaps both but, you feel, not much fun in the pub. If life still seems worth living then walk into a room of Picasso's cubist paintings. Before you get trapped by pointless puzzling about why a woman's right eye is a foot below her left you will, I guarantee, find your heart leap with joy at the vivid colour and cartoon vitality of his creations. Incidentally, the more you discover about Picasso the more you understand why he seemed to see women in various states of distress. From the fact that he was quite likely to seduce a young student in front of his current woman to the fact that it was difficult to walk across a floor in his flat without standing on a tube that squirted paint up your leg life with him was not always easy.

The following day I decided to walk to Montjuïc. This was to be one of the most memorable days of my life. Montjuïc is the name of a hilly area on the coast just to the south of Ramblas. The name might mean 'Mountain of Jews' or possibly 'Mount of Jove' or possibly not. Apparently the name appears in a number of other Spanish towns. It is more a broad low hill than a mountain. It became internationally known when it was the site of the Olympic Stadium in 1992. I knew it to be a good location for a panoramic view of the city. It was also the site of the Joan Miró exhibition. Miró is, I suppose, a little less well known than Picasso, but he was certainly a major artist. I decided to take a long route through the city to see more of its districts. I have to say this was not a particularly rewarding experience since nothing much appears ever to have happened in any of them. My route did not take me past any of the peculiar structures for which Gaudí was responsible, and there was not much sign that any other architect had found inspiration (or perhaps money) there. However, it was a sunny day and I walked along dressed in casual clothes with a light shirt and a jacket. I reached Montjuïc in my circuitous way by climbing the steps from a spot just south of

Ramblas and near the statue of Christopher Columbus at Port Veil which means "Old Port". This area was once thronged with ships, their personnel and cargo. That commerce has moved away from the main city and this area has now been developed as a pleasure centre with cafés, restaurants and other diversions just like pier 29 in New York. The odd thing about the statue of Columbus is that he is pointing to Italy rather than the New World on which his fame rests. I'm not sure if this gesture is supposed to have some meaning like "don't waste your time crossing the Atlantic. Italy's more fun". He did of course originate from Genoa so perhaps this was just a bout of homesickness.

I climbed the steps and made for the Miró Foundation which is well worth a visit. It was opened in 1975 and is as attractively modern and airy as the Picasso Museum is grand and mediaeval. Most of the works on display are by Miró, but other modern artists are also represented (it may not be very accurate to call Miró modern now since he has been dead for some time, but I suppose I still think of everything from Picasso onward as modern). Like much of Picasso and Dalí, Miró's work depicts an odd world inhabited by strange little beings like tadpoles or demented escapees from a junkyard, little pieces of twisted wire optimistically wearing a false moustache and specs in a misguided attempt to look human. Others are simply blobs hovering in the ether observed by an animated inkblot. The colours are usually gorgeous, bright and generous. It is difficult not to smile at Miró's work.

From there I walked along with a great view of the city to my right. I looked at the deserted Olympic Village and then my day really began. I felt my caffeine levels were getting dangerously low and decided to head back to Ramblas for coffee. On reflection, I imagine I could have had coffee in the Miró Foundation but don`t now know why I didn`t. I quickly found one of the paths going back down the hill. It had been generously provided with wooden steps between the low bushes. I was ambling down, looking forward to my coffee when I heard steps behind me approaching rapidly. I idly reflected that someone was in a greater hurry than I was. Perhaps his caffeine need was even more urgent. A young man in his early twenties passed me, and as he did he looked directly at me. I anticipated a cheerful Spanish greeting but none came. On he went in his hurried way. Moments later I noticed that he had stopped at the end of the path, at the landing on top of the two sets of concrete steps that led back to the town. Suddenly, the young man was not in a hurry. He stood looking around him as if wondering how to pass the time. I thought this behaviour odd and decided to keep an eye on him as I passed. I reached the landing and was walking past him when I heard him shout: "Oh senor, the birds." I realised straight away what he was trying. I stopped and asked him to explain. He said "Your jacket, senor, look at it." I took off my jacket and saw there was a substantial brown deposit on the back. His suggestion that this had been produced by birds relieving themselves seemed unlikely since it smelled so clearly of chocolate. In addition, the deposit was so substantial that either one bird had a surprisingly large capacity, or the entire flock had congregated on a piece of targeted bombing scarcely equalled in the annals of warfare. I am no ornithologist but I doubted whether avian intestinal activity in Catalonia was so different from that in Scotland. I wondered if I had stumbled into some Iberian version of Burl Ives` old song which went:

 In the Big Rock Candy Mountains
All the cops have wooden legs
And the bulldogs all have rubber teeth
And the hens lay soft-boiled eggs
The farmers' trees are full of fruit
And the barns are full of hay
Oh I'm bound to go
Where there ain't no snow
Where the rain don't fall
The winds don't blow
In the Big Rock Candy Mountains.

Spanish birds excreting chocolate seemed to belong there. In his eagerness to be helpful my new friend produced an unopened bottle of water and a fresh packet of tissues. Just my lucky day to find someone so well prepared. I laid my jacket on the wall of the landing and, like old comrades, we began to clean it. My new friend carefully patted the pockets, no doubt to make sure they had not also been targeted. Then, in a supreme gesture of reassurance after my trauma, he began to pat me on the back, the shoulders and finally he found the money belt I always wore when travelling. My pockets are always empty on such outings. At this I pushed him away and said "Thankyou, senor, I`ll be on my way." I realised this was the denouement of our encounter. If anything was going to happen it would be now. I now noticed another young man a little uphill who was watching us. As I put my jacket back on I eyed my new comrade. His face was wonderful. It expressed deep puzzlement. I felt he had earnestly studied his correspondence course in mugging tourists but somehow had missed the lesson on how you actually get the money. Perhaps he had been told that the British were so fond of fair play that I would simply acknowledge his supreme skill and decide to surrender my worldly wealth. "You won it fair and square" was perhaps the phrase he had been taught to expect. I walked away, alert to the possibility of footsteps following. I heard none. As I reached the bottom of the stairway near Christopher Columbus I permitted myself a glance back. The young desperado still stood watching me, his face the picture of a man asking himself how it could all have gone so wrong. I wondered how he would face his tutor, his Fagin, admitting that he had not only failed to get any money but had used a new bottle of water and a fresh packet of tissues along with copious amounts of quality chocolate. He was actually in the red for the day`s activities.

As I rejoined the crowds on Ramblas I reflected that my caffeine deficit was now significant, but that I had just had an encounter with Europe`s most incompetent mugger. I felt that was a special moment. My coffee tasted better than ever and I felt the small outlay for a very effective roll-on stain remover was a price worth paying. As I sat in the afternoon sunshine and casually watched the crowds enjoying the many attractions of the city, I almost felt a surge of pity for the mugger. How must he be feeling after failing at an activity for

17

which Barcelona was held in such high esteem? It was obvious that he was not a natural for street crime or even park crime, but to fail so catastrophically suggested he was likely to be completely useless at everything else as well.

That evening I decided to try a restaurant in Calle Santa Ana which had been recommended to me by one of the other guests in the hotel, a Norwegian who was apparently cycling round Spain. I noted that even at breakfast time he looked extremely tired so I assumed he was at the end of his ambitious venture. Not at all. He had flown to Barcelona a few days earlier to acclimatise, and was about to pick up his bicycle that day. It was tempting to suggest he call in at the hospital for a check-up before setting out but it was hardly my place to sew doubt in his mind. I wondered what he would look like by the end if he ever got there. However, I decided to trust his gastronomic judgement and walked the short distance across Ramblas to the eating place. After my demanding day a short walk suited me perfectly. It was a warm evening and the city was displaying that wonderful feature of southern European evenings, families in the street wandering happily along, not shut in at home as we do further north. I was quite hungry and looking forward to eating. Since I have always found Spain to be one of the most reliable countries for good food I had little doubt that the dinner would be of quality.

I was welcomed by a tall young man with a gaunt face framed by a generous beard with moustache. I don`t speak Spanish particularly well but like to try, and consider it a courtesy wherever I go to at

18

least offer some of the language. I said I would like a table for one. I sensed a slight hesitation which I thought strange since I was eating very early by Spanish standards and the restaurant was almost empty. He replied in English; "Of course sir, follow me." I was a little disappointed. If I had wanted to speak English I could have done so, and how was my Spanish to improve if everyone replied in English? He showed me to a table by the window, handed me a menu and glided off to, I assume, the kitchen. The behaviour seemed a little odd but I wondered if perhaps the strange intestinal complaints of Barcelona's birds were affecting him too. If so he had my sympathy. I looked at the menu and after a moment's puzzlement realised it was neither in Spanish nor English. It was in Catalan. I don't speak Catalan. In fact it is not very different from Spanish, particularly if you also know some French, but the spelling is unfamiliar and I was not sure of some of the words. When he reappeared I asked if I could have a menu in Spanish. Again there was this moment's odd hesitation. He took away my menu in what seemed to me a needlessly sulky manner and returned with one I could understand. The reason was that it was in English. As it happened, I really wanted to see what the food was called in Spanish. "Don't you have a menu in Spanish?" I asked in Spanish. I did not pretend my mastery of the language was perfect but I had no doubt at all that it was understandable. I was beginning to suspect what the difficulty was here. He sighed and looked at the ceiling. At this moment I noticed an older man, shorter, dark hair swept back, emerge from the kitchen and hover in the background with a look of some concern on his

19

face. "Sir," replied the young man with a look of frayed patience on his face, "we are now in Catalonia and in this part of Europe we speak Catalan. I can also speak perfectly good English." I could not hide my amusement as I noticed the older man begin to hurry towards us. I took some pleasure in explaining to the earnest young patriot that it had taken me several years to acquire the poor Spanish I now spoke and I had done so as a courtesy to his country. If I could not be served before acquiring some mastery of Catalan then future customers would find the bleached skeleton of a Scotsman at my table, bent over a yellowing book of Catalan grammar. There was no time for me to see the young man savour the full humour of my reply before the older one reached the table and said something to his colleague in what I took to be Catalan. Whatever he said was clearly even less amusing than my comment as the youngster flounced off to the kitchen and, quite likely, out of a job. My new waiter apologised profusely for my reception and handed me a menu in Spanish. He explained that the younger man was his nephew and had decided to become a fervent Catalan nationalist. This part of Spain, which is economically the most successful, has quite a strong separatist movement. I knew something of the political and historic reasons behind this, but felt that indulging my wish to see a menu in Spanish was unlikely to retard its progress much. I haven`t often come across this kind of reaction but I am aware that some Catalans have a strong attachment to their tongue. The odd thing is that it is not unique to Catalonia and really does not mark it out as different. If you travel further south you will encounter the language known as Valencianos which is in most ways identical to Catalan. I have however never been expected to speak Valencianos even in the remoter villages. Go north into France and you will find Catalan there also. My new waiter could not have been nicer or more patient with my attempts at Spanish. I began with "Parillada de verduras" which is much tastier than the translation "grilled vegetables" makes it sound. It was of course then inevitable that I would follow it with fish such as I had seen at La Boqueria. The waiter recommended the dorada which he brought with a carafe of the house white for which he did not charge me. In fact I would gladly have paid for it because the food was excellent and the service ultimately very good. Even the initial disagreement I took as an embellishment to the evening like mustard on steak.

I had still not viewed the works of Gaudí . Others had told me about this wonderful architect and how overawed they had been by the cathedral La Sagrada Familia. I decided to devote a day to him. I set off after breakfast across the majestic Plaça de Catalunya to a street named Paseig de Gracia. This area of modern Barcelona is probably the one I like best. The English word "passage" suggests a narrow thoroughfare, but Paseig de Gracia is as broad and elegant as a Paris boulevard. It has splendid apartment blocks, prestigious shops and a variety of good cafés and restaurants. A few hundred metres along it I came to the first of the Gaudí works, a house known as La Pedrera. Whatever else you might say about Gaudí, his stuff is surprising. La Pedrera, dating from 1905, is colourful and spacious. From the street its lines appear wavy as if viewed through water. Inside, this impression is enhanced with balconies that look like seaweed and a peculiar rooftop where you can wander between dreamlike shapes. It is memorable and amusing. Whether or not you would want your house to look like that is a matter of taste. However, you would not be entirely alone since across the street is Casa Batiló which was an existing house given the Gaudi treatment with a roof that looks like a lizard threatening to jump down on the traffic below. I left these houses still uncertain what to make of this strange architect. Would I want to live in one of these houses? Probably not. Did I think they enhanced the appeal of Barcelona? Probably. Many of its streets otherwise struck me as plain and unimaginative. Gaudí certainly corrected that impression.

I continued along Paseig de Gracia because I was making for Parc Güell. I could have taken the underground or a bus to it but I had time and it was a pleasant day. I stopped for a coffee after a little over an hour in an area that seemed to consist mostly of offices. That, I assumed, was why, when I had emptied my cup, it was whipped away and the table wiped as if I was expected to leave. This was such a contrast to the experience I had had in other parts of Spain that I wondered if this did mark out Catalonia as different. On balance, I thought the particular area I was in was simply more accustomed to thrusting young executives on their way to the next deal than idling tourists too misguided to take the metro when required. I eventually reached Parc Güell and was relieved to feel a sudden affinity with Gaudí. This project had apparently been intended as an up-market property development. It is built in the Gracia area well away from the centre which at one time would have exuded industrial fumes. The wealthy Eusebi Güell moved into a house in the area and invited Gaudí to design the rest of it as a 'garden city' as had become popular in Britain. Ultimately only two houses were ever built on it, neither designed by Gaudí. He did however unleash his strange imagination on the rest, making widespread use of tiles and mosaics, creating lurking lizards and colourful birds' nests along the twisting paths. I thought the place delightful, but evidently the stern bourgeoisie of Barcelona in 1914 or thereabouts had no wish to occupy an estate with smirking salamanders and blue dragons in unlikely spots. Understandable perhaps, but the city's decision to acquire the property and turn it into a public park was probably a good one since it does provide a colourful and imaginative contrast to the city which, to my mind, has an unmistakable austerity about it.

All that was left was the mighty cathedral about which I had heard so much and which I had dimly spied from Montjuïc and Parc Güell. La Sagrada Familia was the last commission of Gaudí's life which occupied, even obsessed, him until he was accidentally killed by a tram car in 1926. I knew that he believed each element of the cathedral had a meaning consistent with his strict catholic faith, and that it was his contribution to reclaiming his countrymen from dissolute ways. He did not have much patience with people admiring it as art or architecture. For him it was a religious statement. It was a longish walk from the park but I intended to compensate for that by having a particularly good meal in the evening.

I find it hard to pinpoint exactly how I felt when I reached La Sagrada Familia and stood looking at the front of it, which is the one part that is almost complete. I stood before an immense frontage topped by multiple spires (there will be 18 in all when finished) whose first impression on me was of melting candles. It was quite unlike any other building I had ever seen. I went inside and up the lift which takes you up most of the 170 metres of the building's height. From there you can see much of the surrounding city, but you can also see that although this project began in 1882 it is still far from complete. I then came down and wandered over the vast site. Some of it is unquestionably beautiful, but often seems more like a homage to nature, with depictions and sculptures of plant life rather than normal biblical references. I have no idea what particular aspects of catholic faith Gaudí wished to depict or invoke, but for me the impression was of a very bizarre and chaotic enterprise. Perhaps when it is finished, if it ever is, some sense of unity will appear. Perhaps for those with a better appreciation of Gaudí, Catholicism, art or something it already is there. I have since visited it again, but my impression was no different. A remarkable building or building project but whether it is an artistic, architectural or theological triumph I have no idea.

That evening I walked to the Barrio Gótico to another recommended eating place which further justified the high regard in which I held Spanish cuisine. It is likely that I am too base and primitive a character to be wholehearted about more lofty aspects of the city.

The following day I took the bus for Girona airport to return home. As I waited I was rewarded or chastised by a phenomenon as surprising to me as La Sagrada Familia. From a sky that could be described as cloudy but not threatening we suddenly experienced a blizzard. Coming from Scotland, that was not a new experience for me. What made it unique was that it was suddenly joined by a violent thunderstorm. The blizzard did not stop. It continued, apparently indifferent to the fact that an entirely incompatible weather system was happily pounding away at the same time. Blizzards I associate with hostile northern climes. Thunderstorms I associate with steamy oppressive southern lands which Barcelona might almost be. As the bus struggled through swirling snow, driving rain and billion volt lightning flashes I wondered if we owed all this to William the Hairy. Had he brought Thor, the Norse god of thunder and giant-slaying to where he properly belonged, but had to accept the blizzards came too? Or was it a more modern vengeance from the skies for my imperfect appreciation of Gaudí.

SEVILLE

Not many of my decisions have been determined or much influenced by grand opera. I have always loved the great arias which I heard as a child. They meant so much to my mother, but I was always content to take the view that it would be wise not to confuse such ecstatic outpouring in any way with reality. Hence, I have never expected females in advanced stages of tubercolosis to perform remarkable feats of lungpower and vocal dexterity, especially not with orchestral accompaniment. Despite the wonderful quartets in Cosi Fan Tutte and Rigoletto I have normally preferred to let someone else finish speaking before offering my own contribution. I have occasionally made an exception for that small but annoying band of people who never do finish speaking however much their audience glaze over, shake their watches, yawn or collapse. So, it was a rare event in my life if not a unique one, that my decision to visit Seville was clinched by operatic considerations. It would no doubt have been on my list of compelling Spanish cities anyway, but this was reinforced by one or two items. One was that more operas have been set in Seville than in any other city. There are the settings of the two plays by Beaumarchais, The Marriage of Figaro and The Barber of Seville. There is Mozart's Don Giovanni and Bizet's Carmen. There is Beethoven's Fidelio. There may be others less well known but these ones are outstanding. I was further intrigued by watching a performance of Carmen set in the actual city, not an artificial backdrop. Early in the action Carmen, the bewitching gypsy girl, appears, coming out of her place of work, a cigarette factory. The building she comes out of looks palatial and I wondered if it really could have been used as a cigarette factory rather than the aristocratic residence it resembled. I had to know. Add to that its wonderful climate, its flamenco music, its association with the moors, the oranges, the spooky procession of semana santa and the mixture was irresistible.

I visited Seville in early March when the temperatures were in the mid 20s Centigrade. I had booked a hotel in Plaza Ponce de Leon, a moderate walk from the old centre. I took a taxi from the airport and the driver, a talkative fellow of around 50, was happy to chatter to me in Spanish which I sometimes followed. He was proud of his city and explained it had, for example, the largest cathedral in Europe. I gently suggested that I thought this distinction belonged to St.Peter's in Rome. He told me that was a common mistake but the important thing to realise was that St. Peter's was not a cathedral but a basilica. I was surprised since I had thought the words interchangeable, although basilica originates from the Greek word for royal and was not originally ecclesiastical. In fact, it appears that "basilica" strictly applies either to the four major churches of Rome or, by extension, to others granted specific papal rights. My driver then went on to boast about the large number of "mesquitas" in the city. This word I did not know but would normally have guessed at the meaning as a particular kind of biting insect. My faith in this translation wavered as he said with pride that

Seville also had the largest example of this in Europe. I rejected an alarming vision of a giant sci-fi monster preying on casual visitors. We passed this "largest mesquita" and I realised it to be, of course, a mosque. The Moorish, Islamic influence was strong in southern Spain so I should have guessed this straight away. This influence is intriguing, partly because of the often negative and confusing images we get of Islam today. The Moors who invaded Spain in 711(at the request, oddly, of the reigning Germanic tribes which could not manage to agree amongst themselves and decided on an arbiter) and spread northward were not racially Arabs as is commonly supposed. They were tribes of Berbers from North West Africa. They had been converted to Islam under duress by the Arab tribes who set out after 622 to conquer everything along the north of Africa and through Persia and Afghanistan into India with the aim of conversion. So, the Berbers did ultimately owe theoretical allegiance to the caliphate in Damascus, but Damascus seemed not to be very interested in this far away country. Eventually a caliphate was set up in Córdoba and Islam in Spain took on its own character. It is worth knowing something of this history because so much of what is glamorous and impressive in modern Spain owes its existence to these Berbers. However, our modern term `barbaric`, like `vandals`, confirms that these foreign visitors did not always have the interpersonal skills we might hope for in visitors. Throughout Spain the language has been heavily influenced by these invaders. Common words such as *naranja* (orange) *aceituna* (olive) and *zanahoria* (carrot) are Arabic or Berber in origin. Hence they are quite unlike their equivalents in other

28

European languages (apart from Portuguese which had the same influence).

I reached my hotel in the early evening. I had watched cookery programmes on TV where some celebrity chef prepares magnificent seafood with aromatic herbs against the backdrop of the Sierra Nevada mountains. With that image in mind I could hardly wait to get out to the city and eat. Whilst some of my most interesting travels have resulted from getting lost in strange places, I really did not want to roam for hours around Andalusia before dining. I studied the map carefully and was confident I knew how to reach the centre rather than dark suburbs. At another time I might be delighted to happen on the scene I have in one version of Carmen where gypsies in the Sacromonte mountains roast a goat which they eat with wild mushrooms. However, it was noticeable in that scene that there were no Scottish tourists struggling with the language and looking for clean cutlery. I might not have been welcome. I will not say more about my evening meal other than that I sat at a pavement table on a busy street and chose from six photographs of seafood with rice. I wasn`t sure I wouldn`t have enjoyed eating the photograph more than the meal. I had always felt Spain was the most reliable of countries for food. I wondered if Seville was going to change that view.

The following day I decided to head for the bullring. I am no fan of bullfighting but my film of Carmen made the Seville Maestranza (bullring) look beautiful in the afternoon sun. This is the setting for the last act of the tragic opera where the splendid but cruel Carmen is stabbed by her distraught lover. Like a *toro bravo* she is a magnificent natural force, but she torments Don Jose as the picadors torment a bull. Don José is as tortured and enraged as the wounded animal and strikes out as desperately in an act that ensures his own destruction as much as that of his beloved. Well, that is opera in all its passionate wildness. I expected a more tranquil day, partly because I was visiting in March and the bullfights did not begin until April.

The bullring is situated beside the river which has the magnificent name of Guadalquivir. It is a useful rule of thumb that river names are like operatic arias. They`re much more romantic if you don`t translate them. This one is no exception. Guadalquivir simply means "the big river". I suppressed that knowledge and enjoyed the exotic rhythm of the Arabic name as I stepped out into the morning sun. I hadn`t seen Plaza Ponce de Leon or my hotel in daylight, so I wasn`t sure whether I was in a world treasure or a slum. In fact it looked pleasingly Spanish and pretty. The streets were narrow but the buildings were white which caught the sun impressively. Occasionally the walls were decorated with *azulejos*, the blue tiles so much associated with the Islamic world of Iberia. The whole scene was brightened further by the red and blue flowers in windows and doorways.

I headed towards the area known as El Arenal, an ancient part of the city once dominated by shipyards and weaponry until the river silted up. Then it became a haunt of brigands and smugglers. In the 20th century the river was

dredged and rendered fully navigable again.
Money was spent and the spectacular bullring was
constructed beside the Guadalquivir. That in turn
brought dozens of bars and cafés to serve the
hordes that love the *corridas* (bullfights) which
have taken place here for more than two centuries.
People sometimes speak as if bullfighting were an
ancient Spanish tradition, arising from prehistoric
times. Not at all. It is relatively recent, and Seville
was its birthplace. You could be forgiven for
believing that the average thinking *toro bravo* (
big wild bull) would not count Seville on his list
of 10 places to see before you die. He might prefer
vegetarian areas like stretches of India. However,
he would have to consider the point that in such
areas he would not be considered a valued member
of society. If he had any life at all it would no
doubt be pulling a cart through mud infested with
snakes and a multitude of biting insects. In Spain,
until the time he is released into the ring he would
have enjoyed a gourmet diet with a sex life the
average British bull could only dream of. Not a
choice I'd want to make, personally, but it's
probably true that a lot of them would have no life
at all without bullfighting. Not for me to say if that
would be good or bad. I have no love for
bullfighting but I have never attended a *corrida*
and it seems to be true that they are accompanied
by far less violence than a typical football match
in Glasgow or Manchester, perhaps because at a
bullfight the whole crowd are wanting the same
outcome, which usually happens as the mighty but
dead bull is taken off to the butcher's slab that was
always his destiny. Even in the rare cases where
the bull wins and slaughters everything in the
arena they still kill him. He'll be on a slab the

following day whichever course he takes. It seemed to me the only workable strategy for him would be to wink at the good-looking ladies in the audience and hope to be adopted as a pet. The window of opportunity would be rather narrow for this approach but you never know.

The Maestranza is a large circular building beside the Guadalquivir. It is brilliant white with red rooftop tiles and neat ochre squares above each of the many accesses. The main entrance, the Puerta del Principe, is a regal, baroque gateway with magnificent wrought ironwork originally designed for one of the city`s convents. Across the road from it is a life-size bronze of Carmen, certainly not designed for a convent. It does seem to me a little sexist that for Spanish males to get a statue they had to write huge novels as Cervantes did or paint miraculously like Velazquez. All Carmen had to do was behave like some of the teenage girls I can see from my window every day teasing awkward young males. In fact, being fictional she didn`t even have to exist.

Although the guidebook said it was mandatory to join a guided tour at the Maestranza I paid 2 euros to a kindly, elegant gentleman with silver hair and a quasi military uniform who told me I was free to wander as I wished. He seemed glad of the company and his soft-spoken Spanish was easy to follow. He was obviously proud of his job and the majestic building he served. He advised me I would find the museum very enjoyable.

I went first out to the huge red circle of death that was the arena (arena, incidentally, is the

Spanish word for sand). The sun was now high in the sky and gave the great silent stadium a blinding brightness. I could understand why the seats in the shade cost twice as much as those in the direct sunlight. There was a pitilessness about the fiery clarity of the light in which it was not difficult to imagine Carmen`s violent end. I recalled also the festival atmosphere of colour, rejoicing, magnificent horses, gorgeously dressed young women and resplendent picadors I had seen in the film as the preamble to the battle. The stadium is very impressive and beautiful but I wondered how many visitors stood in it thinking like myself of music rather than tauromachia, the strange lore of the bullfight about which Hemingway wrote so admiringly. I was thinking rather how much great Spanish music was written by non-Spaniards. Bizet was French and based his opera on a French story by Prosper Merrimée. Chabrier (Espana) and Ravel (Bolero) were also French. The magnificent Capriccio Espagnol was composed by a Russian, Rimsky-Korsakov, along with the other operas I mentioned earlier. I should say that Spain has produced Tarrega, Granados, Rodrigo, de Falla and many others so they are not outdone. Something about the land inspires music.

I went round the museum. I can`t say I found it enjoyable. It struck me as peculiar that so much reverence should be accorded an activity I thought odd and unappealing. Having said that, many of the matadors came from very poor backgrounds. They became very rich as a result of their undoubted skill and courage. As a way of escaping from poverty and of having a life of wealth with the company of beautiful women it

33

was better than becoming a plumber. To that extent I could understand the reverence. As I was considering this, the uniformed usher strolled in languidly and joined me. There was something inappropriate about his gentle courtesy as he described the instruments and clothing of this violent event. I very mildly aired my view that it did all seem a little one-sided to me, although I wasn`t suggesting they should ensure a matador was regularly gored just to even things up. He smiled in the certainty that he had the perfect counter to this. He assured me that sometimes the bull did win and, pointing at the wall to illustrate, when it did win its hide was cured and hung on the wall of the museum to his eternal memory. It was difficult to appreciate what satisfaction the bull would derive from this.

I was hungry now and quite hot. I decided to head towards the Marie Luisa park which was recommended for cool repose. I trusted that I would find an acceptable eating place on the way, hoping that my admiration for Spanish cuisine could be restored after the disappointing meal the previous evening. I wandered along the narrow streets of the old town, enchanted by the little bunches of flowers by the doors and windows of the white houses. A number of eating places looked quite appealing but were not just what I wanted. I reached a square at Puerta de Jerez and immediately saw a restaurant with tables in the shade on a broad pavement. Across the road were palm trees and a little further on was the Guadalquivir. I judged that the couples I saw at the tables were discriminating. The menu was on a lectern on the pavement and it offered regional specialties like gazpacho and fritura de pescados, a variety of seafood fried in olive oil with garlic and lemon juice along with jamon iberico which you find all over Spain. A small, dark-haired waiter nodded to me and indicated a table in the shade which I accepted. Some tall palm trees were behind me and I was able to see both the restaurant on my left and the street on my right. The sky above was clear blue and the midday sun was hot, but sitting in the shade was like easing into a warm bath at exactly the right temperature. He handed me a menu which, I was reassured to see, contained no photographs, and he went off. A few minutes later he returned with a bottle of water, bread and a small plate of tapas, some squid, octopus, olives and onions. I asked him for a carafe of the house red which was a little foolish at lunchtime in a hot country, but it made me feel like a true citizen of the world, an international man of suavity and mystery. I had to allow that no one seemed very interested in the mystery and no important businessmen or diplomats were awaiting my razor-sharp attention in the afternoon, but self-delusion is certainly helped by a glass of Manchegan wine on an empty stomach. I was, however, alert enough to choose my favourite asparagus mayonnaise as starter. I followed that with the fritura de pescados which was exquisite.

I was now mellow and content. The restaurant had totally restored my admiration for Spanish food and I was very satisfied that I had seen the bullring and had managed passable Spanish. This Buddhist serenity might have lasted if I had not chosen a spot that was on the route from town to the University. Little had I suspected the great danger that lay in store for me. As I sat back with my coffee I began to notice little groups of shapely, raven-haired beauties walking purposefully past. They were obviously students on their way to classes. They exuded that wonderful self-assurance that is perhaps only possible when on the threshold of adulthood. With their dark eyes and their olive skin they too were part of the enduring legacy of the Almohads, descendants of an African world imported like spices from far places. These young ladies were likely to know opportunities their parents could never have imagined. Spain was hurtling from a backward age into sophisticated modernity and their horizons were greater than those of any Spaniard since the conquistadores. I watched them and felt my Buddhist peace dissolve into dissatisfaction. Gone was my Nirvana so briefly and deliciously glimpsed. I was sitting in that delightful restaurant with excellent food, warm Iberian sunshine, the exotic splendour of Andalusia and no companion. Little chattering groups of Carmens were striding past and my inner Don José was mesmerised by them. I glanced at the small amount of wine in my carafe and unfairly blamed it for the evaporation of my tranquillity.

This was a phase when the euro had been diving south even faster than I had. The bill when it came was ridiculously cheap. I paid it and set off again towards the park, still restless and unsettled. I crossed the road and began to walk beside the spectacular Alfonso XIII hotel. It was just one of a number of magnificent buildings that reminded me that Spain had once been the richest country in the world and Seville had been at the heart of that wealth. I was just reflecting on how much more tastefully it had spent its money than some other centres of commerce when my thoughts were disturbed by the sound of someone shrieking. The sound was entirely out of keeping with the general calmness of my day. I wondered if turning the next corner would become a matter of regret for me, but I did it. Ahead of me, the street along the longest side of the Alfonso XIII hotel was deserted apart from two people. One was a very small woman and the other a very tall man. The shrieking sound was coming from the woman. My initial thought that she had stubbed her toe or messed up her hairstyle were obviously not adequate for the situation. She was howling with surprising energy in German at her tall companion who appeared to be her husband. I had no wish to get any closer to them but they were directly in my path for the park. Short of a spectacular and perhaps life-threatening plunge into the Guadalquivir I had no other way of reaching my goal, so I proceeded. I gathered that something for which he had been responsible was *schrecklich* (dreadful) and *unglaublich* (unbelievable). I had, however, missed the substance of the complaint. It was tempting to stop and ask her if she could give me a quick resumé of what I had missed so I could put this performance in context. Had he groped the chambermaid, failed to appreciate her hairdo or simply left the Spanish phrasebook in the hotel? None seemed to catch quite the intensity of the moment. I came nearer to them and walked past without their showing the faintest sign that I existed. I quickly stole a look at the man`s face and realised that he would at that second have traded everything to be rid of his companion and have the solitary tranquillity I had been so foolishly regretting.

I walked along, the shrieking continuing, having moved I felt into a minor key as Beethoven sonatas do when a more reflective phase overtakes the great man. Was a little voice within the lady finally asking if this was really the best possible way to appreciate Seville? Had the tall man collapsed at her feet in a fit of squirming misery, momentarily tugging at her iron heartstrings? Did she have a sore throat? Had he perhaps found the Spanish phrasebook? I would never know, and the question was swept from my mind as I happened upon another majestic building which, strangely, I recognised. In a joyous moment I realised that this was the tobacco factory from which the mischievous Carmen had emerged. She too had tormented a man but not by blasting his eardrums. She had awakened his impossible dreams and her method was ultimately much more deadly. So, was it a tobacco factory indeed? As I stood there, little groups of Carmens like those who had passed the restaurant came and went. They were students. It was part of the University of Seville. However, a notice beside the gate explained that this had indeed been the Royal Tobacco Factory at one time. Only later in my visit would I understand why such a fine building had had such an apparently unworthy purpose.

One block further and I reached the park. Straight away I realised why the tourist guides praised it so highly. Wide avenues of mature, broad- branched trees offered immediate shelter from the hot sun. Sweet perfumes from the warm south hung around shrubs and wafted gently around me. I walked until I reached a lake in the centre of the park. Ducks and swans drifted along on it and an island in the centre had a small gazebo. The warmth, the wine, the lunch and the exercise had all gently eroded my drive and sense of purpose. I was a little surprised that more people were not enjoying this oasis. There was no one in sight.

My northern restlessness gave way to the mood of a lotus-eater and I gratefully sank onto one of the benches by the water. I envied the ducks that could paddle their feet in coolness. However, I resisted the miasma of idleness gradually taking hold of me. I opened my bag and took out the sketchpad which, by now, contained inept drawings of many parts of Europe, some almost recognisable. I took out a pencil and gazed languidly around for an appropriate subject. I had decided the little gazebo was no great task for a man who had tackled the Palazzo Publico in Venice and the Uffizi in Florence. The fact that I had abandoned both in exasperation was not relevant. The gazebo looked to be just about my standard. I did some rough measurements to get an idea of proportions and tried to decide what I would include. One of the biggest tasks for someone sketching a garden scene is how to simplify. The amount of detail is overwhelming, so much of it has to be ignored. I was just applying myself to this task when my attention was distracted by a `plop` sound as if something had fallen from the trees. I didn`t pay too much attention. I turned my thoughts back to the gazebo

but then heard another `plop` and then another.
Something was falling from the trees behind me. I
couldn`t imagine what it might be, but I tensed a
little as I remembered a story told by a great uncle
of mine who had once stayed in a beach hut in
Bermuda. He too had heard regular `plop` sounds
during the night. On lighting a candle in his cabin
he had noticed with horror giant black spiders
walking along the beams above him and landing
on the floor. Was this why the park was so quiet?
Did all of Seville know that the unwary traveller
enjoying nature would soon be surrounded by
armies of tarantulas which would have little
interest in his unrecognisable sketches of
European treasures? With a supreme act of will I
turned, steeling myself for the horror that might
even then have been sidling revoltingly towards
me. Of all the occasions in my life when I have
been an obvious idiot this one has a special place,
a gold medal, Oscar winning, supreme triumph of
buffoonery. What I saw falling noisily onto the
empty pathways was not giant spiders or any other
nightmare incarnate but the product for which
Seville is more famous than for anything else. Not
Carmen, bullfighting or the Guadalquivir. Seville
is famous for large, delicious oranges. The best of
marmalades which I had often eaten with delight
was made with Seville oranges. If I had had the
alertness of a Sherlock Holmes or even the
ordinarily awake traveller I would have noticed
that lots of the branches along the avenues were
heavy with the large, ripe fruit. I could have
harvested the walkways and made a year`s supply
of marmalade. I blamed the wine, the heat, the
distraction of the Carmens, the demented shrieking

of the outraged Frau, my descent into the mentality of the lotus eater.

After another very good meal and a sound sleep I woke excited about exploring Seville further. I had decided I liked the city very much. Of course, it was the old city I was exploring. I knew there was a thriving modern Seville around this historic centre and I had no doubt it contained many things of interest but they were not in my sights. For those who know something of the city's history and feel my romantic excitement naive I should just say that I was well aware that the tranquil park I had visited on my first day had been the scene of some of the most hideous outrages of the Inquisition. I knew very well some of the atrocities of the Civil War period. I had no illusion that bullfighting was the cruellest of the happenings of this city's past, but what enchanted me was the beauty and grandeur that had survived all that, the style and the beauty of a people who were now enjoying democracy and prosperity. The various religions and political movements that had tried to dictate how people should act and believe could all very well hang their heads in abject shame, but human vitality, creativity and good sense were triumphant. Of course, people could lament that some kind of ethnic purity was being corrupted by tourism, but I have little patience with unspoilt places. They are usually cold, dangerous or uncomfortable with very few chances for a good meal, a leisurely chat or entertainment. I like spoilt places.

I headed for the Giralda which I now knew to be the tower of the largest cathedral in Europe.

It too was only a short distance from the river in that old city of narrow streets with whitewashed houses that suddenly opened into grand squares like the one occupied by the cathedral. It stands on the site of a mosque built by the Almohads, one of the powerful Berber tribes who brought Islam to Spain. I find it intriguing how each of these creeds happily makes use of the other's holy sites. Since they were often condemning each other as antichrists and infidels should they not have been avoiding the space contaminated by the other? Or is there some truth in the old belief that such areas were chosen for the spiritual emanations detected by soothsayers and other purveyors of august mumbo-jumbo? I could not deny that I too was deeply impressed by the majesty of this great edifice in the Iberian sunshine. Perhaps I was deceiving myself to believe it was only the grand architecture that was affecting me. I went in and wondered at the space, the artistry, the grandeur. I have always felt I was only saved from some ecstatic experience at that moment by the fact that two groups of tourists were being shown round. One was oriental, Japanese I think, and the other German. Cathedrals, churches and mosques are capable of providing a sense of awe, reverence and stillness which are hard to find elsewhere in modern life. That is a most valuable effect and is better not tarnished by claims that it is only available from this brand of belief or that. However, no heresy or infidel can ever break the mood quite as effectively as a guided tour. The leaders of these delegations appear to be appointed largely for their penetrating voices and ability to avoid breathing for impressively long periods. Mercifully, many of them have now been replaced by handheld sets which communicate only with the purchaser. I was not able to understand the Japanese guide but listened for a time to the German. She poured out facts about the Moorish belltower, the minaret of 1198, the renaissance belfry of 1568 and the iron grills protecting the majestic capilla mayor, a wall of gold in the main chapel. All of this was available from a guidebook and of negligible importance compared to the opportunity to absorb the stillness and timelessness that were available to us. Looking at the faces of the tourists I felt my cry would not have found an echo. As if the guides were not making enough noise the tourists chattered to one another, some while devouring chocolate bars. A voice told me it was morally wrong to look down on people who had a different way of appreciating the great edifice. Another voice told the first one it was an idiot.

I made my escape by climbing the many steps of the Giralda, the bell-tower, hoping not to be followed. I emerged to blue sky and warm sunshine. I looked over ochre and white coloured buildings interspersed with palm trees, the great river that had risen as a trout stream in the Sierra Cazorla near Córdoba and now wound to the sea, the maestranza, the theatre, the park and the wonderful water gardens of Reales Alcazares which would be my next visit. I realised that few cities had spoken to me as this one was doing. I can't say that what I was feeling was a sense of belonging. It was all too different from my homeland. Yet I felt a profound appreciation for so much of what I was seeing. I suspected that whatever it was that spoke to me was also the reason so many French, Austrian, Italian and Russian composers had found inspiration here.

It was a short walk from the cathedral to the Reales Alcazares or Royal Palace. This dates from the fourteenth century when Pedro I decided to create a royal residence from the palaces left by the Almohads. Craftsmen arrived from Toledo and Granada to create a masterpiece in the *Mudejar* style. Colour, coolness, elegance and practicality all combine in the palace, still used at times by the Spanish royal family. The gardens illustrate the reverence the former desert dwellers felt for water and just as in the Alhambra in Granada or in Córdoba water is used like an artist's material to create fountains, water jets, cascades and pools all surrounded by trees and bushes to provide shelter from the hot sun. I wandered along the shaded avenues, appreciating the delightful sound of water in motion and felt a kinship for people who could create such a haven. Our word "paradise" is ultimately derived from an old Persian word for a garden or walled enclosure which encourages tranquillity. The word predates the Abrahamic religions of the Middle East but comes from the same part of the world as the Sufi version of Islam which has provided much of its poetry and charm as for instance in the Rubaiyat of Omar Khayyam. I thought of that poem in the magnificent English translation of Edward Fitzgerald and felt in the cool avenues by the sparkling water under a blue sky that I was very close to that world of one thousand years before.

I'm not sure what would ever have moved me from that nourishing retreat if I had not been driven by my desire to see more of this great palace. I particularly wanted to visit the Salon de Embajadores, the hall of the ambassadors. Although Islam appears to me a little dogmatic in forbidding the use of images in its art and architecture the resulting use of colour and design does often give a great sense of peace (the meaning of the word Islam) especially as compared to the endless crucifixions, martyrdoms and joyless madonnas featured in so many Christian places of worship. I have difficulty finding anything spiritual or uplifting in scenes of blood, torture and mutilation. The dome of the Salon de Embajadores is a wonderful expanse of gilded, interlaced wood that draws the eye and the spirit as if to an infinity of light and immensity. Different artists of different periods have contributed to these marvellous palaces and it was here that I understood at last the mystery of why Carmen, the cigarette girl, emerges from a building that looks fit for a queen. In the Reales Alcazares you can see the plans used by Christopher Columbus and the subsequent conquistadores. These explorers, funded by Queen Isabella, explored the New World and brought back treasure. In strictly monetary terms one of the great treasures was tobacco. That did much to enrich Spain so it was not surprising that it should be dignified by such grandeur.

I had done a lot with my day and I was now hungry for a late lunch. I decided to cross the river at Puente San Telmo and walk back to one of the string of open air restaurants that lined the river. I chose one that was just across from the Maestranza bullring and sat at a table shaded by a parasol.

From here I could see the Guadalquivir a few metres away from me and I could admire the impressive buildings along its far side all bathed in strong sunlight. Looking down the river I could see on the far bank the Torre del Oro or golden tower. This sizeable round tower was built in 1220 and had a twin on the opposite bank, long since demolished. Between the towers was a massive chain that normally lay beneath the water but could be winched up to form an effective barrier to unwanted shipping. The building is now a maritime museum and is no longer golden, if it ever was. It is thought it may have been decorated with golden tiles at some stage. That would have looked magnificent in strong sunlight, although probably a considerable hazard to modern driving.

My waiter was again serious as had been the one at Puerta de Jerez. He was older, perhaps a little over fifty, with some difficulty in walking. However, his face eased into a gentle smile as I tried my imperfect Spanish. He advised me that the anchovy starter was a favourite with some people, but its strong flavour was not to everyone's taste. He thought I'd enjoy the octopus in garlic and olive oil if I normally enjoyed that type of dish. For the main course he thought the swordfish was the best of the fresh sea catch available as long as I enjoyed quite a `meaty` type of flesh. I had eaten swordfish before so I knew what he meant. Previously I had eaten it `meaty` but succulent and other times `meaty` but more akin to a slab of mahogany than anything that had swum in the sea. I trusted his judgement and sat back to look at the graceful scene. The sun was very pleasantly warm. I poured my first glass of white wine and relaxed, looking forward to my meal. Across the Guadalquivir I could see the statue of Carmen beside the bullring, the essence of hot passion and the torments of desire. Further downstream I could see the Giralda and the dome of the Reales Alcazares, great sublimations of human energy to hint at a supreme peace when all passions had stilled. Around me I saw the activity of human life that pulsated between these extremes like the electricity between the anode and cathode of a battery. I was pleasantly aware that for one of the rare occasions in my life I was in a state of equilibrium between these poles. It was one of these times when I was conscious of being happy. My waiter returned with my starter. He smiled a little more easily. I felt he trusted me now as someone who was happy to enjoy his country's cuisine without complaining that the fish was not the way we did it in Glasgow. My struggles with his language were a leveller between us, acknowledging that his imperfect command of English was no small feat.

After this delightful meal that again cost less than a pint of beer in Scotland I went back over the river and wandered past the Torre del Oro in the region known as El Arenal. This was the area in which stood the bullring but now I took my time, enjoying the beautifully white walls and admiring the less famous churches. I also walked past a house with a plaque to Miguel de Mañaras. That name probably means nothing to most people, but it takes on more meaning when you know he is often credited with being the original of Don Juan Tenorio, the legendary lover. It seems that Miguel was something of a charmer who kept

47

the company of many of the ladies of the city in the 17th century. Allegedly his life was changed when he had a vision of his own impending death. This led him to a new life of philanthropy rather than philandery. He founded the Hospital de la Caridad which one can still see in the Calle Temporado.

After this, although there was much still to be seen I felt I had achieved most of my aims for my first visit to Seville. I already had a great deal to savour and reflect on. There was only one vital project remaining. I had to attend a performance of flamenco. Flamenco is a remarkable creation, born, apparently of a fusion of gypsy and Arab traditions. Its roots were quite probably, like jazz, in the creativity of gifted but relatively untutored musicians and dancers. It has developed into a worldwide passion with more flamenco schools in Japan than in Spain. It is now a complex, highly intricate art which demands great natural ability and considerable training. I asked at my hotel where I could see a good performance. He gave me an address in the Calle Maria Auxiliadora and told me the performance began at 10.30. He had tickets so I bought one for the following evening.

I looked forward to my evening`s adventure and at 10.00 I left my hotel. This turned out to be a more daunting outing than I had expected. The narrow streets with the white walls and the flowers that I had appreciated in daytime were now dark alleys. The evening family sorties I so admired in southern Europe were over for the day and the streets were largely deserted. There were bright lights in the city centre but I was walking away from it into suburbs. I had a map and there was just enough street lighting for me to make out where I was, but unfortunately Calle Maria Auxiliadora was just the name for one part of one of the longest thoroughfares in Seville. It was tempting to turn back and find a taxi, but I decided it could not be terribly far. Once I joined this long, dark road I walked for a few minutes in the direction I thought most probable when I saw ahead of me some movement of people going into a building on the right. I hoped that might be my destination. I took heart and hurried on. With relief I saw this was it. It was a small theatre.

I entered the foyer and a slim man in a waistcoat who, in a Hollywood film would be a shady croupier, gestured towards a black curtain. A middle-aged couple were just going through so I followed them. The auditorium was small and dark. I found my seat. Attached to the back of each seat was a small table. Another slim, croupier type came unsmilingly towards me and placed a glass of red wine and a bowl of tapas on my little table. I thanked him and he nodded gravely. I gathered there was a certain gravitas deemed appropriate to flamenco. It reminded me of what I had heard of the Bayreuth Festival theatre in Germany dedicated solely to the works of Richard Wagner and attended by devotees with mystical adoration. It is no doubt mere hearsay but I have been told that once the doors at Bayreuth are closed for an Act of one of his music dramas there is no escape. No urgency of bladder or migraine is sufficient to warrant release. If you have the misfortune to have your coronary then you are expected to have the good grace to await the interval before going to meet your maker. I assume that is malicious gossip and I really did not feel as confined in this little hall. Others slipped quietly in and by 10.25 I could not see an empty seat.

Soon on the dark stage we were aware that figures had taken their place but they were mere shadows at this point. There was a deep hush as we waited. Lights went up and we saw scenery which suggested perhaps a mountain village. Two men sat on a low bench to the left with guitars. One was around thirty, lean with very dark hair. The other had a more square face with equally dark hair just beginning to recede. His face had deep lines by his mouth and his eyes had the intensity of passion and hardship. He looked very gypsy. In the centre of the stage was a slim young woman with black hair severely tied back but falling around her shoulders. Her olive skin looked dark in the stage lighting and her eyes, like the older guitarist`s, seemed to be gazing at some inner turmoil she could barely contain. She wore a gorgeous orange dress that hugged her slender torso and fell in generous folds around her legs. They were all motionless while every sound in the theatre ceased and we waited with true urgency. Slowly, deliberately, the older man picked up his guitar and struck the strings furiously. Then he began the strange, intense, wailing type of singing that is at the heart of flamenco. The younger man followed with powerful, angry rhythms as if years of intensity were finally being released. Slowly the dancer tapped her heels on the floor, every move passionate, wrestling with the emotion, seeming to draw it painfully from the air or from her soul. Her pace quickened and quickened until we were in the full flow of her wonderful dancing and the majestic guitar rhythms.

I was captured by the performance and the two hours of it passed quickly. Like so much of Seville, the very strangeness and alien nature of flamenco seemed to speak very directly to something in me. Why? I could ask, but was this not why flamenco had become popular at the farthest ends of the earth. I was a little surprised at the end to see the performers smile and laugh with friends in the audience. Now they were relaxed, sociable, untroubled. Where had all that pain and intensity gone?

I had achieved all my aims and could now just admire and appreciate. On my last evening I decided to look for an up-market restaurant. The ones I had patronised so far had been excellent, but amazingly inexpensive. It was not that I longed to spend more money. I was simply intrigued to know what a bigger outlay would provide when the quality I had experienced so far had been so good. I have never adjusted to Spanish dinner times. It is not unusual for a Spanish family to begin their evening meal shortly after I have gone to bed. However, the Spanish have adjusted to tourists. I did not want to go out again after dark on deserted streets. It was much more pleasant for me to walk out while the shops were open and the streets busy with leisurely evening strolls.

I headed for the area around the Cathedral, the Santa Cruz district, sometimes referred to as the old Jewish quarter. There had been a thriving Jewish community in Spanish cities like Seville, Cordoba and Jaén under Muslim rule. After

Christians reconquered the area Frederick III confined the Jews to this quarter, admittedly now perhaps the most attractive. In 1502 a piece of legislation called the Alhambra Decree exiled all Jews from Spain. Most found their way to the city of Thessaloniki, now the second city of Greece, then a major city of the Ottoman empire. There they played a major, although not always harmonious, part in one of the most civilised parts of Europe for hundreds of years.

I walked happily through the narrow streets, still warm in the evening sun, rubbing shoulders with young Spanish families, older couples taking the air and tourists like myself. I soon found myself in the Calle de las Sierpes ("street of serpents", none of which was in evidence), passing shops selling goyesca dresses, wide-brimmed Spanish hats, veils, fans of all sizes and colours, castanets, mantillas (the lace head dresses) and all sorts of souvenirs. At the bottom of this street there is a plaque marking the site of the former royal prison whose most celebrated inmate for a short time was the great Don Miguel de Cervantes Saavedra, author of Don Quixote.

In one of the quieter side streets I noticed an entrance to a restaurant. It had the blue *azulejo* tiles on the walls and dark mahogany tables on terracotta floors. It looked cool, clean and inviting. It had an unassuming nature as if it felt no need to advertise its quality. I took this as a sign that it was known to those who could appreciate food. I went in. A young waiter, round face, dark hair, dark eyes welcomed me in English. I explained that I liked to practise my Spanish, imperfect though it was. He smiled pleasantly and accepted that. He showed me to a table, saying something that was completely unintelligible to me. He could tell by the look on my face that I had not understood a word of what he had said. We both laughed. I asked him if he would be good enough to repeat it in Spanish but more slowly. Of course he would. This time I understood that he was asking me if I wanted to sit indoors by the window or outside since there was a garden terrace. I asked if he thought it would stay warm outside. He felt that it was still a little early in the year and that I might be uncomfortable when the sun went down a little more. We agreed that I should sit indoors by the window where I could look out at the sunlit garden while that was possible. He asked me where I was from and we had a short conversation in which I could tell he was speaking with particular care to help me to follow. I knew there was a strong Andalusian dialect which he probably used in his normal speech but I heard few traces of it and I was grateful for that. Andalusian does not claim to be a separate language as Catalan and Galician do but it is distinctive and is probably the form of the language that has most influenced American Spanish, perhaps because of the large number of people from the poor region of Estremadura who braved the Atlantic journey.

The waiter brought me a menu in five languages. I was grateful because this enabled me to learn some more words. If I read the menu in Spanish then I could check anything I did not understand in the English or French versions. This admirable idea was however disappointed. I looked at the seafood dishes and saw *besugo insalata, lubino insalata* and *dorada insalata.* I knew that *insalata* simply meant "with salad". I knew that *dorada* was gilthead, a fish I have often eaten on the continent but have never seen on a British menu. I turned eagerly to the pages in English to read "besugo with salad, lubino with salad and dorada with salad." I asked the helpful waiter if he had any idea what we called these fish in English but he didn`t. He was surprised to learn that lubino and besugo were not English words. I decided to trust Spanish cuisine and ordered besugo. I began with calamari in garlic and olive oil which was delicious.

I was the only customer in the restaurant for a short time. After about fifteen minutes I was joined by four Americans, presumably husbands with wives. They were all probably around fifty and showed some evidence of coming from a land where large food portions are not unknown. I confess to being a little rattled at their entrance. Their voices were loud and they were indifferent as to whether or not I was at that moment in deep meditation, although, to be fair, it was probably perfectly obvious that I was not. One of them, a tall heavy man with a round face and spectacles called to the waiter: "Say can you bring us some of your red wine. Hell, I don`t know. Any red wine you would drink yourself will be fine. Carl, would you rather have a beer? They`ll have beer. You`re not going to get your oatmeal stout here, boy, but.... hell no, we `ll stick with the wine." The waiter complied and helped them to choose a beef casserole that, they reckoned, was about as near as they could get to the food at home. They made no attempt to speak Spanish and I am ashamed to confess that I was experiencing a very European attempt to fit American visitors into the unflattering stereotype that was all too common.

I finished my starter and my own bottle of Spanish white arrived. I began to drink it, realising that one or the other of the Americans would glance at me from time to time as if wanting to find out my story. I tried to appear invisible. My besugo came and I realised it was sea bream. Only later did I discover that the word, rather appropriately as it happened, is also a Spanish word for an idiot. Once I had got over the loudness of the Americans I could not help picking up some of their conversation. Some of it was amusing and I had to acknowledge that I rather liked the fact that four friends had come all this way and were so unrestrained about their enthusiasm. I began to eat my sea bream and it was delicious. I was just having another sip of wine when one of the American women turned to me and said: "Excuse me, do you speak English?" I smiled and admitted that that was my native tongue. She went on: "I'm just so interested that you are eating fish. I've wanted to try the fish here and I really haven't known what to go for." I told them that in my opinion it was all first class. We chatted further and I learned that they came from Columbus Ohio. It was their first time in Europe and they were so excited about the whole trip. They thought Seville just the most beautiful thing they had ever seen. I became increasingly ashamed at my resentment of them as they won me over with their enthusiasm and friendliness. They were so impressed that I spoke Spanish, but of course they did not know enough to realise how imperfect was my mastery of it. As we spoke I reminded myself that their country was much larger than all of Europe and that I had, at that stage, still never crossed the Atlantic. I looked at my besugo and wondered whether the idiot was what was on my plate or the man who was eating it. I had spent much of the week despising the immense intolerance of Christians for Muslims and Jews in the history of Seville and I was not performing much better. In addition, it was easy for me to be quiet and unobtrusive when I was alone. If I had been fortunate enough to have the congenial company they had perhaps I would have been a little noisy also.

I had only spent a week in Seville but I felt it would take me a long time to absorb and digest all that I had seen. Few places have ever impressed me more. I had been confronted on my last day by my own stereotype of a certain kind of American traveller. In my own defence I would say I had met many from the USA throughout Europe who were quiet, erudite, appreciative so I was by no means hostile to Americans. However, I had permitted myself to take the initial loudness of these four as implying other unattractive characteristics. I had been wrong. In Seville I had become acutely aware of how useless were other stereotypes, ancient and modern, whether of Spain, of Islam or of Jews. Judging by the media and conversations in everyday life it seems to me that the tendency to blame and condemn those different from ourselves is as much alive today as ever. It appears to be a very difficult lesson to learn that people are people.

TOLEDO

Toledo is one of the most astonishing and important places on earth. I don`t suppose that is generally realised, but it is true. Only Venice, I think, when approached from the lagoon, can match the impact of one`s first sight of the old Spanish capital. A half hour train trip from Madrid brings you to a railway station like a small Moorish palace. You walk out and see this ancient, majestic city covering a cone-shaped hill. At the top, dominating the scene is the ancient Alcazar or Palace. Around it are spires and towers, each with a colourful history. At the foot of the hill, all round it, rages the twisting, restless Tagus River like the giant serpent in Germanic legend, protecting the immense cultural treasure that is Toledo. You are in no doubt that this visit will be a very special experience. Again, like Venice, despite its tiny area, a mere 90 square miles (232 square kilometres) its influence on human life has been immense. You probably do not realise it, but whether your delight is eating marzipan, studying the profundities of Plato, wearing damascene jewellery, clanking around the house in suits of armour or trying to become a Japanese samurai your debt to Toledo is great. It had other important contributions to humanity and civilisation which I discovered.

I had been prepared for some of that. What I had not been prepared for was the strange experience that every road in Toledo is uphill. I had booked into the Hotel Sol and I had to go uphill from it to reach the old city. I assumed therefore that returning to my hotel would be downhill, but it

57

wasn`t. It was uphill too. The city was like these drawings by Escher where a man climbs six flights of a staircase only to be back on the level he started from. I found myself becoming resigned to this. I began to wonder if the entire city was a gravity hill like the famous "electric brae" at Croy in Scotland which so puzzled President Eisenhower. On the electric brae ("brae" being a slope) you drive to this stretch of road in south west Scotland which is obviously going uphill and yet if you switch off the engine and release the brakes the car will slowly climb the hill. It is one of the spookiest driving experiences available. It is in fact an illusion simply created by the unusual configuration of the surrounding landscape. You are actually going downhill. Of course, my experience in Toledo was also an illusion, but a strong one. Perhaps because the uphills were so steep they lingered longer in the mind. I marvelled at the numerous elderly people in the city who must simply have accepted that life was one endless uphill climb. Their conception of heaven was presumably a world where the road occasionally went down.

For this reason it may be wise to visit Toledo alone. I could see it as a major source of marital disharmony that your day`s shopping would end with yet another relentless climb. Indeed, I suspect this was the true reason why Felipe II decided to move his capital to Madrid in 1561. His wife may well have rebelled at every outing ending with an hour in an oxygen tent. Alternatively, not to be sexist about it, perhaps she was an athletic type and Felipe could think of no other way of escaping from the torture of his Sunday morning stroll.

Certainly, a short city walk in one of the suits of armour for which the place is famed would be a memorable cardiovascular experience.

Like so many Spanish cities, Toledo had been a settlement long before the Romans came and used it as a major metalworking site. It became a capital city first of all in the sixth century in the kingdom of the Visigoths. They were a Germanic tribe which migrated from Eastern Europe, probably driven out by the Huns from Siberia. Those who moved west were known as Visigoths and the others as Ostrogoths.

When I left the station in very Spanish sunlight, Toledo looked more a product of another age, another world, another way of being than anywhere else I've been, with, as mentioned, the possible exception of Venice. One of the reasons for this impression is undoubtedly the absence in each case of suburbs. If you enter Rome or Paris by rail or road you will pass through modern featureless areas that could be in any European country. When you reach the part that is unmistakably the great historic city you piece its grandeur slowly together. Not so with Toledo. Come out of the station and that august, very Iberian amalgam of Europe, Africa and the Middle East is there on the hill in its majestic entirety. More even than "the eternal city", Rome, it is another age living on quite heedless of the passing centuries.

I crossed the bridge over the writhing Tagus river and began my first climb up to the small hotel I had booked. There was something very appropriate about this ceaseless climbing. From the Alcazar at the top down to the swirling river Toledo announced itself as being on a higher spiritual and aesthetic plane than a mere human being could ever aspire to. Onward and upward had never seemed more necessary.

After my first breakfast in the city I walked up the narrow cobbled street to the Puerta del Sol (Gate of the Sun). Whether as homage to the sun or to use up excess building materials this gate has a double Moorish arch and two towers. Although from the Visigoths onwards the various regimes were nominally Christian or Muslim it`s tempting to imagine many of their secret prayers were more directed at our natural source of heat and light. In mid- summer you would have begged it to cool down and in winter you would despair in the Manchegan winter of its ever returning. I find it hard to believe that concerns about vicarious atonement or the doctrines of the Caliphate held quite the same sway.

Those not in prime Olympic condition might want to pause at the Puerto del Sol since they will probably just have climbed a steep hill. Their excuse can be to look out at the wide, arid plain of La Mancha which surrounds the city. If they are imaginative, or just a little affected by oxygen debt after the climb, they may just see the faint spectre of a gaunt figure in battered armour trotting along on a knockkneed, malnourished horse. By his side there would be a more rounded figure on a patient donkey. These might appear because the Knight of the Woeful Countenance, Don Quixote de la Mancha set off from this arid plain on his clapped out horse, Rosinante, with his unfortunate

60

companion, Sancho Panza, in the rich imagination of Don Miguel de Cervantes Saavedra, the greatest of Spanish writers. This wonderful novel is certainly as true to modern life as to ancient. Don Quixote was able to deny all common sense and practical evidence in his compulsion to interpret everything according to his crazy world view. Determined always to do the right thing by his absurd chivalric standard, he created mayhem and disruption all around. All setbacks or surprising events were seen as the work of the Great Enchanter who had to be confronted in the cause of Virtue. The mindset of many from Hitler to Mao to Al Qaeda down to the petty tyrants of hospital wards, businesses and trade unions is no different, if often even more disastrous. Don Quixote has immense stamina for beating his head against brick walls before understanding finally dawns that his world view is crazy. Perhaps a thorough grounding in Cervantes' great work would prevent lots of distress and injustice, but probably not. Human beings cling very desperately to ridiculous beliefs. It is very beneficial to wonder at times if one might be wrong, but it's not a common human trait.

I went through the Gate of the Sun and, like time travellers in fiction, I stepped into an ancient world, but one which has gratefully accepted some features of modernity. A few steps from the gate you reach the Plaza Zocodover. This has been the practical heart of the city for centuries. Its name, from the Arabic *Suk Al Dawab* means "animal market" and that's what it used to be. However, it has changed its use somewhat to the more profitable, if scarcely less messy, business of

61

feeding tourists. Tables with parasols cram two sides of the square and the illusion that you are in a modern city is enhanced by young waiters with American accents. They learned much of their English from Sesame Street.

I pushed through this square on my first morning and plunged into the alleys of the ancient city. I was heading for the old Jewish quarter which has in fact been empty of Jews since 1502 in the same xenophobic rage that expelled the Muslims in 1492. This brought to an end a period when Jews, Christians and Muslims had lived together in relative harmony and to mutual benefit. The Jewish merchants had brought a range of goods without equal in the mediaeval world. The synagogues remain as works of great beauty which unashamedly borrowed features from the Islamic mudejar architectural style. The Islamic world had brought the genius for architecture and design that still draws admiring tourists in huge numbers. Perhaps of even greater value, they had Arabic versions of the great works of classical literature whose originals had been lost in Europe`s many upheavals. It was a culture which gave scope to highly cultured and erudite men such as Ibn Rushd, better known to us as Averroës. Although his name may not be very familiar now he was a remarkable polymath who profoundly influenced both Christian and Islamic thought. Indeed the Christian school known as scholasticism was largely based on his work and became for a time perhaps the most powerful influence on Church thinking. Those who have admired the works of Homer, Plato or Sophocles have these great scholars to thank. The Christian world in its advocacy of the Prince of Peace destroyed that prime example of culture and tolerance and replaced it with the Inquisition. They too should perhaps have read about Don Quixote.

I thought of this as I made my way along the narrow streets beside great buildings. Even in late April there were crowds of tourists drawn by this ancient world. I, however, was on my way to an area on the edge of the Jewish quarter, to a house which looks over a steep hill that runs down to the Tagus below. The house stands at the edge of the Plaza del Conde and is famous for its supposed former owner, Domenicos Theotokopoulis. The reader will readily understand the difficulty even learned Spanish priests might have had with this alien name. Posterity has remembered him by the nickname given by the locals, for he is the celebrated painter El Greco, "The Greek". Domenicos was born in what is now the Greek island of Crete. Then it belonged to the Venetian empire. His fabulous talent could not get fulfilment in his native island so he travelled to the then mighty city of Venice and soon after to Rome. Whatever other talents Domenicos had, charm appears not to have been one of them. Great artists have often been misfits. He may not, like Caravaggio, have occasionally murdered people or, like Beethoven have hurled bowls of pasta at them, but in general people seem not to have been sad to see him go. It can't have gone down very well in a Rome that was intoxicated with the genius of Michelangelo Buonarotti that El Greco not only appeared unimpressed by the great man but even offered to paint over his work in the Sistine Chapel to do a better job of it. Perhaps it is no surprise that he felt it would be wise to leave Rome.

Spain appears to have been his last hope on his westward itinerary and that didn`t begin well since Felipe II didn`t much like his painting. So, if you are a great Cretan painter and the king of wherever you are doesn`t want your work what do you do? You`ve tried the Doge of Venice and the Pope so what`s left. France can`t stop tearing itself apart with civil war and England involves a long sea journey to a cold island where the king (Henry VIII) has a tendency to chop heads off and upset the Pope (possibly, on reflection, giving him something in common with Domenicos). Since the expulsion of the Jews there are few rich merchants in Spain whose egos could be flattered with lavish portraits, and we have no record of pavement artists being in fashion in Toledo at the time. Where would Picasso have been if there had been no market for depicting prostitutes, clowns and triangular women? Well, Domenicos was lucky. Perhaps he had exercised unusual foresight. He had gone to Spain as many of his Italian contemporaries did to see the art in the Escorial palace near Madrid. While there he got a commission to paint an altarpiece in the church of San Domingo El Antiguo. The king was running short of painters since some of the best in Spain had died and neither Titian nor Tintoretto wanted to come from Venice. However, Felipe didn`t like his work much. Two things then worked in El Greco`s favour: politics and ecstasy. The politics arose from the fact that the secular power of the king was matched and sometimes opposed by the might of the Church. Sitting amid the cathedrals, converted synagogues and mosques of nine centuries the church fathers were not amused by Felipe II's decision to move the nation's capital to Madrid in 1561. They needed a propaganda victory. Otherwise the sackcloth and ashes they preached might have become a humiliating and uncomfortable, reality. The ecstasy which played its part was not substance abuse in the Toledo disco, but, apparently, the real thing. The mighty figures of St Theresa of Avila and St. John of the Cross had written magnificent accounts of 'the mystical experience', an allegedly direct awareness of absolute truth which they attained through Christian practices. Probably no one was more astonished than some of the priests to learn there was actually some truth behind the endless tracts of dogma they pretended to believe. The poetic, lucid accounts of St. John's "Dark night of the Soul" and "Flight of the Alone to the Alone" came from a man who had suffered extreme privations for his beliefs. However, these works were only available to the literate and educated. Painting and sculpture could announce truth or propaganda to the uneducated. Domenicos Theotokopoulis brought from Crete a knowledge of eastern iconography and a remarkable sense of colour and drama. His gaunt, ethereal Christ and disciples visibly gasp with bliss, and if his depiction of the Holy Land or Paradise looked surprisingly like Toledo then the message was powerful and complete. The king had moved, but truth and ecstasy were to be found here in Toledo, there for all to see even if they couldn't read.

The city still celebrates El Greco, and the house which he may have lived in is spacious with a wide courtyard. Its stone benches and flowerbeds make it a marvellous place to enjoy the spring sunshine or drink wine with friends or a lover on a balmy evening. I always find it striking and a little sad that great artists who often struggled for a crust of bread become on their death a provider of great income and employment for their chosen city or town. Wars are the same. Poor soldiers have died in their millions in Europe over the centuries, leaving destitute widows and children, and yet now their graveyards and battlefields draw wealthy tourists in huge numbers to provide local employment and affluence.

I wandered around the house and courtyard for a time in the sunshine. I tried to engage the serious looking caretaker in conversation about El Greco but she had either scarcely heard of him or regarded tourists as unworthy recipients. I felt she had only a fragile relationship with ecstasy. I wondered how nostalgic he had been for his homeland of Crete where you are rarely far from the sea. Toledo is in the centre of Spain so he would have had a long journey to reach the Atlantic or the Mediterranean. He did usually sign his paintings with his name, followed by "Cretan" so that designation was important to him. However, he appears to have had a comfortable lifestyle in his adopted city. He was admired and esteemed by his patrons, the church and he had a Spanish lady friend, Jeronima, whom he probably never married. She did, however, provide him with a son, Jorge Manuel. He was nominally a catholic which was no doubt prudent. His biographers believe he never wavered from his Greek Orthodox upbringing, but, at least to the outsider, its practices don't differ very obviously from those of Catholicism.

I returned to Plaza Zocodover for coffee followed by excellent tapas, a Spanish omelette with some cuttlefish. I then headed through the Archway of Blood which, for once, led downhill. This chilling title came from the Brotherhood of Blood who offered consolation to those about to be executed in the marketplace. I tried to imagine as I passed through the archway what could be seen as consolation by the impending victim: "You'll never have to pay another electricity bill"; "Just think, no more toothache"; "You'll never have to climb another hill". I assumed the offering would be a little more theological, but since the Church seemed to do a stronger line in hellfire than heavenly peace I felt they might be well advised to avoid the subject.

Just below the arch was a bronze statue of a man as gaunt as an El Greco saint but with a look more of worldly wisdom and imperfection than ecstasy. If El Greco had imbued his work with spiritual truth then here was the master of worldly truth, for this was the great Cervantes who, allegedly, had stayed at the Inn of Blood beneath the arch when writing one of his tales. In any event, Toledo is now the administrative capital of La Mancha, and Cervantes had spread its renown throughout the world and the centuries with Don Quixote.

I continued downhill, following little alleys and stairways until I reached the San Martin bridge which enabled me to cross the turbulent river. From this location I had a different view of the town from the one I had had on leaving the station.

I was now looking up towards El Greco`s house with the Alcazar towering above it. It was an impressive sight. From that view Toledo has an immense air of self-sufficiency, even an indifference to anything outside of it. My sense of wonder was slightly tempered by my awareness that I was going to have to climb back up these hills before long.

The descent had not taken long but the return was different. Despite previous disappointments, I still had faith in my sense of direction. I took care to plot an infallible shortcut back to my hotel. Of course I should have learned in this most religious of cities that it is not given to humans to be infallible. More importantly, I should have learned from getting lost in most of Europe and elsewhere that devising shortcuts was not my strength. I spent much of the afternoon climbing little streets which led to other little streets which must have been taking me gently downhill because I was soon climbing again.

On my first evening I walked through the dark lanes to the Calle Comercio under a silver moon that watched me with the cold, unblinking eye of unbending ecclesiastical authority. Towards the end of it I found an eating place. There was no one in it other than a disconsolate young waitress. Sitting amid some of the greatest treasures of mankind did little, apparently, to lift her spirits. I gathered she was only doing this job to pay for visiting a Dire Straits concert in London. She told me her real favourite was Slash, the picturesquely named guitarist of Guns and Roses, but he was evidently an unpredictable gentleman who was not becoming more reliable with age. I felt she had some difficulty in grasping why I, who lived within driving distance of some of the greatest concert venues of Rock music should be wandering the dark streets of out-of-season Toledo. I have asked myself why, even at her age, rock concerts seemed like noisy, messy and expensive affairs without any appeal. I wondered what El Greco would have made of Slash.

The following day I visited the cathedral and the church of San Tomé with its close El Greco connections. As so often, the size, beauty, the intricacy and creativity in such buildings filled me with more of a sense of reverence and awe than words preached in them could ever do. I have felt the same in mosques such as El Miharab in Córdoba, in synagogues and in stark, humble church buildings in remote parts of Scotland. What I and, no doubt, many others, have felt is the same. We probably could have done without the clerics who pretend it`s all different.

I went back to the Plaza Zocodover for coffee and considered the strangeness that Romans, Visigoths, Almohads, Jews and Phoenicians had all found this small area of land so magnetic when vast tracts of the world have been attractive to no one. No doubt Toledo`s situation in the middle of Spain with good weather and the river so near is explanation enough. However, there was another major element in this city which I was still to encounter, but was shortly to stumble upon.

After coffee I wandered aimlessly through the streets. Any one of the churches or the wonderful museum could have occupied me for days, but most of us have limited stamina for such detail and I was as interested in the way people lived and earned their living in the city of today. As I stumbled around in hot sunshine, my direction more dictated by finding shade than unearthing treasures, I found myself in a small, neat, very Spanish square. It was the Plaza del Consistorio. Occupying the far side was a building the colour of pale sand. It had two rows of four windows, one row above the other. Each window was identical, like an arch in an Arab palace with a lattice work wall coming almost halfway up. The wall between these windows was textured as if made of thick pile carpet in brick sized rectangles. On the top of the building were six upright lozenges acting as pillars. Between them ran a series of small arches to form a barrier, except between the two central ones, where the wall was solid with a circular motif like a stylised rose. The building held my attention partly because it was not one of the city's great monuments. Nor was it in a prominent position, and yet style and taste had been called upon to make a very attractive façade. Below these windows on the ground floor were two shops side by side. One bore the legend "Damasguinados" and the other "Ceramica". From where I stood I could see that the window of the first was full of swords and daggers fanning out in careful display. There was also a suit of armour. Toledo still does very well out of its traditional crafts, and the most special and intriguing is that of damascening. The name obviously derives from the city of Damascus and it refers to the highly intricate art of weaving gold or silver into other materials. The material can be the steel of a sword or suit of armour. It can be woven into fabric or other metal for jewellery.

It can be woven into wood as I had seen in the ceiling of the Reales Alcazares in Seville.

I had seen plenty of suits of armour in my life in draughty Scottish castles or museums, but I had never seen one in a shop. Of course I knew something of Toledo's reputation for swords and armour. From the earliest times its metalworkers were famed for producing weapons of incomparable quality. Their method of tempering steel appears to have been very special. The process was, I gather, even copied, incredibly, by the Japanese to make their Samurai swords. I have always been puzzled by the claim that his sword is "the soul of the samurai". I am always suspicious of these bizarre translations from the Japanese. I used to know a Glaswegian who was a former Professor of Japanese. I asked him if the books on Zen which claimed one must transcend or destroy the ego were really translating what the original said. I have met a few people who have claimed to have achieved this transcendence, but they seemed to me more self-absorbed than most of us. The learned professor smiled and explained that such phrases were bound to be mistranslations. The nearest you can come to translating our concept of individuality into Japanese really means selfishness. The western concept of a personal soul is meaningless. If the term "the sword is the soul of the Samurai" has any meaning, it is simply that the Samurai has surrendered all other aims to serve his master with his sword. Not perhaps a very noble aim to our minds. However, I digress.

I went into the shop and I felt something about me told the proprietor I was an unlikely customer. He was a lean, distinguished looking man with a scholarly air. He was friendly and clearly an enthusiast. I asked if he really found customers for his suits of armour and he assured me that he did. "People love Tradition", he confided. I knew this to be true since my own country, Scotland, does good trade in selling traditional dress. However, I felt there was an important difference. I had been at weddings where everyone wore the kilt and plaid. Guests danced, embraced, sat on each others' knees and managed various degrees of intimacy, even falling drunkenly into bed together. I felt a suit of armour would be a serious impediment to all of these activities. As he explained further, I gathered that the typical client was a very rich individual with a huge house in Texas or Japan or Bavaria. Having paid out staggering amounts of money on architects and building materials, he (or she) then had to decide how to fill the thing. Evidently, the occasional suit of armour propped in a corner was just what was needed. Even if I had that kind of wealth I doubted it would appeal to me. The prospect of having to empty it periodically of stubbed- out cigarettes or worse was deterrent enough.

I left Toledo in a strange frame of mind. It had been a very special experience and yet I felt I had penetrated its inner nature less than with any other city I had visited. Its traditions of military and ecclesiastical discipline and its very impressive craftwork could not fail to make an impact, and yet I had struggled a little to find its human heart. In a city so full of spiritual matters I felt I had not found its soul. As I walked back to the station on a beautifully sunny morning I looked back. For a brief moment the city, rising, cone-like, to be crowned by the Alcazar, resembled an austere cardinal or sultan drawing his robes around him. The display was all. The inner core was not to be revealed.

MADRID

I suppose the complete confirmation that Madrid is a very different city from the old capital, Toledo, came on our first full day. I had travelled to Spain`s capital with my friend, Audrey, a good companion and an elegant lady. Ironically, we were crossing Calle de Toledo on a warm sunny day and I was little ahead. The streets were quite crowded and I turned to look for Audrey. I knew her sense of direction was far better than mine, so I didn`t think she had got lost, but she did have a tendency to stop at shops or flower sellers without alerting me. After a moment, I noticed her talking to a man. It was not at all unusual for her to get into conversations with complete strangers but I felt there was a little more to this. She was smiling so I was not too concerned, but I could see her looking around for me, so I went closer and waved. The man looked at me, said something to Audrey and walked off.

"Found a friend?" I asked. She smiled.

"I`ve just been asked out to dinner tonight."

"Really? I didn`t know you had friends in Madrid."

"I don`t. We were just crossing the road at the same time. He said he liked my leather trousers and would I have dinner with him tonight."

"I warned you about these leather trousers."

74

"They don`t have the same effect in Edinburgh."

"So, are you tempted?"

She laughed.

"He`d have to like me for more than my leather trousers."

I could not imagine such an event in Toledo. In reality we had known from our arrival on the previous evening that Madrid was different. We had arrived quite late at our hotel in Puerta de Toledo and thought we were probably too tired for dinner. We both felt a short walk and possibly a glass of wine would help us to get a first sniff of the city and get rid of the stiffness of travelling. I no longer know which road we took, but we were heading for the centre. It was a warm evening, and after crossing a noisy boulevard we found ourselves in pleasant streets where people were strolling and shops and restaurants were still open and busy.

Soon we came to a bar/restaurant that we thought especially bright and welcoming. We went in. Behind the bar was a young, dark-haired man with Spanish style beard and moustache. He was smiling as if having a good time. He welcomed us. I asked if it was all right if we just had a glass of red wine. It would not have surprised me if they had only wanted dinner guests at that time.

"Of course, of course, have a seat. What wine would you like?"

I asked what his house red was. In fact they had several. One was a Garnacha which I had recalled being praised in a recent magazine. I chose that. We sat at a table near the window so we could see people stroll by. Our attention was caught by some tapas displayed on a table near us.

"I might like some of that Spanish omelette," I said

"Thought you weren`t hungry."

"Not sure I am, but that looks good."

"OK then I`ll have some too."

The barman appeared with a carafe and two glasses.

"Actually, we only wanted one glass each," I said.

He shrugged.

"That`s OK. I charge you for what you drink. No more. "

We ordered some of the Spanish omelette which he served straight away.

"That`s delicious," said Audrey. "I think I`m hungry after all."

"Me too."

We finished that and decided we might want a taste of the other tapas if they were as good. We had the equivalent of a decent meal each and finished the carafe. We strolled back feeling content and decided Madrid was a good city.

Breakfast the following morning was a buffet where all kinds of cheeses, cold meats and bread were available. There was also cereal and dishes of scrambled eggs, bacon etc. We found a table and a short, round-faced waiter came up to us with a notepad.

"May I have your room number please?"

I told him.

"May I know whether you would like tea or coffee?"

I had tea and Audrey coffee.

"May I know whether you come from Scotland?"

"You know our accent?"

"Of course. May I know whether you want us to ignore all this rubbish and bring you porridge with big fat sausages?"

He asked this with barely a change in his facial expression, just the hint of a mischievous gleam in his eye.

"Is that what you ate in Scotland?"

"Every morning. I was glad to get back to Spain." He then smiled at us." I joke. I liked Scotland. Very nice, friendly place but we do better breakfasts."

"Well we'll go with your breakfast this morning and then decide."

"Very wise man."

We set off in warm sunshine after breakfast. Audrey still looked good but she was not wearing her leather trousers on this occasion. We crossed to Calle de Toledo and walked again to the centre. We had decided to visit the famous Prado Museum. It is unquestionably one of the world's greatest galleries. Neither of us liked going mindlessly from room to room in museums, so we decided to restrict our attention to the works of Velazquez who, although from Seville, had become court painter in Madrid, revered by the king, Felipe IV, who much preferred watching Velazquez paint to running a problematic country in problematic times. Later we were going to see Picasso's Guernica in the Reina Sofia modern art gallery which was not far away. We were not in a rush. Madrid is a very pleasant city for strolling. It has wide boulevards with lots of trees and open spaces. It had been used in the eighth century by the Moors as the site of a fortress to facilitate the defence of the much larger Toledo. Its name comes from the Arabic word, *Mayrit*, meaning a wall or fortification. Later, the rulers of Castile favoured it as a centre from which to pursue their hunting pleasures. Today it seems like an elegant, spacious, modern capital. The decision which was no doubt controversial in 1561, to move the court to Madrid now seems inevitable. Toledo is a wonderful, unique city but not at all suited to being a modern capital.

Frankly, we didn't give the great Velazquez the attention he deserved. The Prado is so pleasant we strolled through its bright, airy galleries and then, as soon as we thought decent, went for coffee. Our subplot for the visit was to find the best coffee in the city. Less intellectually demanding than reading about Las Meninas, but we took our coffee seriously. The café area was modern and the coffee excellent. I was very conscious even on this first full day of a different atmosphere from the other Spanish cities I knew. Barcelona had been more hurried with the sense that everything was urgent. In Seville there were layers of history and tradition going back to pre-Roman times with echoes of the ancient Tartessus people who had probably been Phoenician. It had been a rich melange of influences, with the Almohads, the Jews, the stories of Carmen and Don Juan, the powerful sense of Islam at its most exotic and attractive. Toledo had been such a world apart with its magnificent buildings and crafts from an age long gone, but with a powerful presence even yet. All of these cities and, indeed, all of Spain, is still trying to deal with the effects of the terrible civil war in 1936 and the tyranny of Franco that followed it. Franco was by no means detested by all Spaniards. In the years since his death many have looked back on his reign with nostalgia. Apparently you have the same phenomenon in Russia with sentimental fantasies about how good times were under Stalin or Brezhnev. This has caused severe tensions in Spanish society and the strong, often bitter rivalry between Barcelona and Madrid owes a lot to these troubles. Of course, many people are only aware of that as football teams vying for pre-eminence, but behind that rivalry which is normally far from friendly are deep historic and cultural enmities. It is very difficult for countries to put civil war behind them. The troubles of the former Yugoslavia illustrate that all too graphically. Even in the United States whose Civil War ended in 1865 there are bitternesses. The economic problems that have hit Europe since my last visit to Madrid have awakened some of these tensions. The whole continent of Europe has spent far too much time at war with itself to the benefit of no one. I hope the beauty, energy and optimism I have seen throughout Spain triumphs.

On leaving the Prado we decided to head for El Corte Ingles, a marked contrast to the world of Velazquez. Audrey had heard about it but had never seen one of their stores. It is the largest department store chain in Europe, and it has branches all over Spain and now in Portugal also. It was founded in 1940 by a tailor named Ramon Areces who had learned about department stores when working in Havana, Cuba. The main one in Madrid is not far from the Prado so we decided to explore the practical after the cultural. Its branches carry a huge variety of stock of all types. The staff are smiling and efficient, the displays are colourful and inviting, and the food served in the restaurant is very good and excellent value. Its success has been well earned. Again this was a modern, comfortable Spain, no longer inward-looking at its own historic problems. This may seem frivolous, but its importance can hardly be overstated. It is a very deep human tendency to divide the world into "them"(the bad guys) and "us"(the good guys). Spain has had its full share of that. It had the

80

divisiveness of the Christians against Muslims,
both against the Jews, the Church against everyone
who could possibly be accused of heresy, the Civil
War, Franco against anyone who disagreed with
him (not unlike the Inquisition) and regional
conflicts which die down in a time of prosperity.
They rise again when times are hard, although it
does appear that perhaps the lunatic Basque fringe
have finally given up. Then Spain suffered the
appalling outrage of the bombing of the Atocha
station in 2004 by another lunatic fringe who
called themselves Muslim without any apparent
familiarity with the teachings of Islam. Against
that background it was a delight to walk through
the sunny streets of the capital and the many
departments of El Corte Ingles and see good
humour and peaceful activities. For bringing
people together commerce usually triumphs over
idealism every time.

It wasn`t long however before we did
explore regal splendour. On paper the Royal
Palace looked impossibly immense. In reality it
looked even more so. It sits in Calle Balen,
overlooking the Rio Manzanares and can easily be
reached on foot from the city centre. It has over
three thousand rooms, and is the second largest
palace in Europe after the Louvre in Paris. It is the
official residence of the Spanish royal family, but
they normally prefer the more modest Palacio de la
Zarzuela on the outskirts of the city. I have never
visited Versailles which was the model for this
after its predecessor had been destroyed by fire in
1734, but I imagine it is equally difficult to take it

seriously. Felipe V of Spain had been brought up in Versailles since he was a Bourbon and was known to feel that the previous Madrid palace was a poor competitor to Louis XIV's extravagant construction. In the gigantic dining room I tried to count the number of chairs at the endless table. Every time I reached 48 or thereabouts some crowd of American globetrotters, Japanese businessmen, British housewives, German historians, Italian philosophers, Mongolian herdsmen or misdirected Inuit fishermen bundled past me. It seemed as if the entire planet was viewing the palace at the same time as us. All I can be sure of is that there were seats for at least 120 people at this table. It made me think of Facebook where you could have 120 friends, most of whom you would not recognise in the street. It was largely the conception of Felipe V, but Carlos II and IV indulged a taste for the manically extravagant also, such as a porcelain room where the walls and ceiling are covered in green and white porcelain. More practically, it had its own pharmacy. I wished I had time and freedom to examine the recipe books to see what medicines were prepared. After holding dinner for 120 people I imagine headache remedies were in demand. Audrey had more of an interest in textiles, marquetry and ormolu than I have and spent some time on them. I wandered around rather aimlessly wondering why anyone would want such a palace. I was aware of the adoration with which Felipe IV of Spain had watched Velazquez at work, evidently much more taken with the majesty of artistic creation than with trying to run an empire. The paintings left of him show a rather sad, bleak individual. I felt that was probably a view common

82

to monarchs leading artificial lives, with no true freedom and probably with no true friends or love that is worth the name. Building outrageously opulent palaces was probably a desperate attempt to give some meaning or purpose to their lives. It was also something to boast about when you met your family members who ran other European countries. Having such a monster palace with 3,418 rooms probably also meant you could invite all of these relatives without running much risk of actually bumping into them. Considering how often in my small house I manage to lose my car keys, mobile phone or address book I wonder that anyone with that number of rooms can be sane.

That evening we set out to try our luck at finding another good eating place. We had noticed what appeared to be a traditional inn under an archway on our way back from the Palace. It seemed so unpretentious and basic after the Palace that I think we were drawn to it as compensation. We managed to find it again. The menu on the wall outside looked rustic but varied, so we decided to risk it. Inside it looked just like a film set for a hostelry from crusading times. The oak beams on the ceiling were massive but looked thousands of years old. The tables were heavy and wooden, sturdy rather than stylish. Two men sat on the right by the window with tankards of beer. I could easily have accepted them as the local blacksmith and saddler for any film about Robin Hood, Don Quixote or El Cid. To the left were two young couples of the backpacking variety, Australians who had no doubt dealt with Vietnam, the High Pamirs and the Khyber Pass on their way. A young blond man came towards us. He was of sturdy build and had a broken nose, but he had a very bright, welcoming manner. Audrey told me he was very handsome. He was clearly the waiter, possibly even the owner. He indicated a table just to our left and gave us menus. We ordered a carafe of house red. He nodded and explained that since it was Thursday they had *Cocino Madrileño*. I had heard of this. It is a traditional stew normally with a variety of vegetables, chickpeas and various types of meat: beef, pork belly, chicken and black sausage. It takes a long time to cook and for that reason is usually only available on one day of the week. If we had wanted hearty traditional Spanish cooking we had clearly come to the right place. The stew appealed to me but we were both also very keen to have white asparagus with mayonnaise. It is difficult to get good white asparagus in Scotland and this was a particular favourite with both of us. It was not on the menu but he confirmed they had some. Audrey thought the *cocino* sounded daunting so she went for the *pollo al ajillo*, chicken cooked in garlic with a white wine sauce, another specialty of the area.

The following day we went to the fantastic Thyssen-Bornemisza Museum. It stands at the end of the Paseo del Prado and is just a short walk from the Prado and the Reina Sofia. The collection was begun in the 1920s by the Baron Heinrich Thyssen–Bornemisza and was continued by his son Hans Heinrich. It was gifted to the nation in 1992. It contains more than 800 paintings and is certainly one of the most important private collections in the world. Allegedly, it was begun by Baron Heinrich when many American millionaires were suffering from the Great

Depression and had to sell off their collections. His son continued it and in 1985 the baron married a former Miss Spain, Carmen Cevera, who has remained closely involved with the collection. It is significant for all sorts of reasons, but one is that it supplements very well the two neighbouring galleries, having important items where they are weak. We decided to look at some of the more modern paintings, by which we meant ones after around 1850. We looked at impressive work by Edward Hopper and Karl Schmidt-Rottluff as well as ones which made us scratch our heads more by Andy Warhol and Robert Rauschenberg. These are not particularly modern now, but still provoke these endless discussions about "is this art?" The discussions go on because it`s not like discussing whether something is a kneecap or a traffic light. If you have never defined the word there is no way to answer the question.

Of course we went to the café and had some difficulty in deciding how it compared with the one in the Prado. The coffee was excellent in both and the ambience probably equally agreeable. We felt no more compulsion to decide that matter than whether Warhol`s tin of beans was art. I did feel Michelangelo would think it a little disappointing that he needn`t have lain on his back for twelve years painting the Sistine Chapel when he could simply have nipped down to the supermarket for a tin of beans. Nonetheless, we can be fairly sure that however artistic Warhol`s tin may be Pope Julius II would have been understandably disappointed.

We had a less frivolous discussion of modern art when we went to the Reina Sofia Gallery to see Picasso's Guernica, undoubtedly one of the great works of the 20th century. The Spanish town of Guernica was bombed in 1937 by German pilots flying in support of the Spanish Nationalist party. Its symbolism is puzzling at first, although stark even on first acquaintance. However, it pays to spend some time understanding it. It is a very powerful statement, a majestic silent cry of outrage that innocence has to go on suffering from the brutality of uncontrolled power. Again it was a sobering backdrop that reinforced our satisfaction at seeing the self-confident, smiling face of modern Madrid. It also reinforced our awareness that the brutality is never far away and the processes of democracy, however imperfect, are the best means we have found of keeping it chained.

Audrey wanted to see a flamenco. I had seen one in Seville and found it memorable. It is of course very Spanish. It has colour, drama, passion and great artistry. I was very pleased to go to another performance of it. We discovered that the Café de Chinitas was in Calle de Torija, a moderate walk from our hotel. It holds some of the best displays in the city. Fortunately we were able to get a reservation for the 10.30 performance. Madrid has, we gathered, some excellent flamenco schools, although it is a style that is mainly identified with Andalucia in the south. Although we didn't have time to explore this point I have read that every type of Spanish cuisine is also available in Madrid, whether it is Galician, Basque, Aragonese or whatever. It would be splendid to have the time to visit and savour each region, but for most people life is too short, so it is good to be able to sample the art and food of every part of Spain in its capital.

We arrived relatively early. We were shown into a hall with a quite a low ceiling. The lighting was subdued. It differed from the venue I had visited in Seville which was a theatre with small tables for a glass and tapas. Here there were tables for four or more being set and at the far end was a stage still in darkness. We took our seats, face to face, side on to the stage which was only 20 yards away. For a time we seemed to be the only customers, and the staff paid us very little attention. Could we have got the time wrong? Were they all going off home and leaving us looking at each other in the dark?

"At least I'd like a glass of wine," said Audrey a little bleakly. She was not at all the type to complain but I sensed the flatness of disappointment from her. She had heard about drama, colour, passion and mesmerising dance. She wasn't seeing any of that. All she was experiencing was a gloomy hall with shuffling noises in the background and no indication that anything would ever happen there again. I wanted to say something reassuring but I couldn't think of anything. There was no point in saying: "Don't worry, it will start soon," when I had no more information than she had. Suddenly, a small, stout older couple shuffled in. They were no more like flamenco dancers than I am like Usain Bolt but no dancers were ever more welcome. As they muttered to each other and fussed about with handbags and jackets we watched them with adoration. Someone else in Madrid believed something was going to happen here this evening. Shortly after that two younger couples arrived. We breathed again. Others trickled in and then a waiter appeared with a basket of bread and some tapas. He lit a couple of small oil lamps on our table: "Would you like some red wine, white wine or something different?" he asked in good English. We eagerly opted for red wine and allowed a sense of excited anticipation to creep back in.

There were three tables between us and the stage. By the time our wine arrived two were filled. The one beside us was still empty. Anticipation intensified more when we realised something was happening in the darkness onstage. We had our first sips of wine, had some tapas and felt content enough to chat about our day. A little later two couples arrived, probably in their late forties. One of the men was tall and lean with hair slicked back and heavy rimmed spectacles. The other man was a little shorter with thin-rimmed specs and very white hair along with a healthy suntan. The women were both blonde and looked as if they had also spent some time in the sun. The two men sat at the same side of their table as I was of mine with the women facing. I guessed they were British or German expats until they spoke. The taller man looked around, directed his attention at Audrey and said: "Say, can you tell us what we`re in for here?"

Like me, Audrey hadn`t really understood what was behind the question.

"You mean the food? We don't know. We've not seen a menu yet."

"So we get food. That's good." His companions agreed. Then the woman next to Audrey turned to her and said. "But is that it? We get some food and that's it?"

We were puzzled.

"Well then the dancing starts," I said cautiously, still not grasping what they were after. The taller man turned to me and said.

"Dancing? Hell, are we expected to get up and dance? I'm still sober you know."

"It is a flamenco performance," I said, again rather uncertainly. The four of them looked at each other in silence for a moment and then burst out laughing. The smaller man, roaring with laughter, said "Flamenco, Dolores, flamenco. You ain't getting' a flamingo."

Although we still didn't understand what was behind this we couldn't help joining in their hilarity. When that subsided they explained they had just got off a plane from Florida about three hours before. A taxi had taken them to their hotel. They had then asked the tax driver to take them out somewhere Spanish for the evening. Dolores, who had dealt with Cubans in Miami, knew some Spanish but not much. She had gathered they would get Spanish food and wine and something colourful with flamingos. They agreed if they hadn't all been a little tired and jetlagged from their journey they would have realised that anywhere in Spain flamenco dancing was much more likely than any encounter with flamingos.

We liked these visitors and gathered Dolores was the slightly taller woman sitting beside Audrey. She was married to the taller man, Seymour. The shorter woman was Marlen (apparently that was the spelling) married to the white –haired man, Norman O. Schransky. They all lived in Miami, Florida and had been planning a trip to Europe for some time. Whereas I, after a long flight from the US, would be sleeping off the jetlag they did not want to waste a minute of their visit.

"So, how long are you spending in Madrid?" I asked, intending to pass on tips like where to get a coffee or, for the ladies, the advisability of wearing leather trousers if they wanted different company from Seymour and Norman.

"We leave in the morning," said Norman, smiling at our astonishment.

"So you flew in here today," said Audrey, trying to grasp this, "and you're flying back to Florida in the morning. That's a hell of a night out."

This led to more hilarity. They explained that they were not going back to Florida in the morning. They were hiring a car and driving south. Both of the wives believed their family had originally come from the south, Marlen from Andalucia and Dolores from Estremadura. Since they all wanted to visit Europe, this seemed a good plan. However, that was not the whole story. They also wanted to visit a number of the vineyards of Spain. As Seymour explained, if you live in Florida and want to see vineyards it's as quick to come to Spain as California. In fact, he went on, there are some good wineries in Florida and in neighbouring Georgia, but they knew them well. In fact Florida was probably the first place in the States to produce wine. French Huguenots had found Muscadine grapes near St. Augustine, America's oldest city, in the 16th century. That was still the grape used in most of the 16 wineries they knew of in the state. So, they expected a very different wine experience in Spain.

By this time food had arrived. Some of us had paella, some the *rabo do toro* or "bull's tail stew" which is hearty and spicy. The conversation flowed and we were having a good evening. It was almost an annoyance when the lights went up on the stage and the performance began. Yet it didn't take long before, the rhythm, the colour, the artistry and the passion of the performers had us all captured. It is part of the great skill of the dancers that every movement of every finger is given meaning. I found myself as captivated as I had been in Seville. I was pleased to see that the others were also enthralled. As before, I was struck by the contrast when the earnest, passionate expressions of the troupe gave way to relaxed smiles between the pieces. No doubt all performers do this, but I had never seen it so strikingly done before.

It became quite a late night but a very good one. The food, the wine, the wonderful dancing and the company of the Florida four all worked together for a memorable evening. We wished our new friends well and hoped to meet up again sometime. If, by any chance, they may be reading this then I hope they are pleased to be remembered.

Sunday was to be Audrey`s last day in Madrid before she flew back to her family. I was staying for another couple of days. We decided to do something rather different. El Rastro is the famous flea market of Madrid. It has existed since the 19th century and is held mainly on two streets running from the Plaza de Cascorro. It was a warm, sunny day and the market was a short walk from the hotel. Audrey wanted to buy something a little different for her children and I was happy to wander around. I have been in flea markets in several cities and many of them are just a pale memory of the bustling commercial event of former days, but El Rastro is different. From the time we approached Calle de la Ribera de Curtidores we could see that this was a major outing for many Spanish families. Large groups of them wandered along in the sunshine. It was soon obvious that this was an important event. We saw stalls ranged as far as we could see, and people milling about enthusiastically. We had visited a smaller market the year before in the Portuguese Algarve, where I had bought some excellent shoes at a very low price and Audrey had found a range of items to take back. We had found some of the traders at that market to be not obvious candidates for sainthood. I particularly remembered the aging ruffian who sold me the shoes. His dull eyes spoke of an intimate acquaintance with cheap alcohol, and the scars on his neck and hands spoke of a life not always spent in perfect harmony with his fellow man. The traders at El Rastro looked quite different. Some were very smartly dressed and spoke eloquently about their produce. Many were still quite young and gave the impression of being eager young business folk. There were the usual stalls for jewellery, scarves, pashminas and shirts. Others had beads, thread and knitting needles, and others had food hot and cold, sweet and savoury. What astonished us were the stalls selling large items of furniture. Heavy tables, wardrobes and chairs were for sale and I wondered how you took these items home once you had bought them. The choice was bewildering, and the excitement infectious under the blue Spanish sky. After a while we were tempted by some tapas and good coffee at a makeshift café where there were seats and tables. Eventually, Audrey bought rather more than she had intended and I got a red denim shirt for 3 euros which I still wear some years later.

One reason I stayed on when Audrey went back to Scotland was that I wanted to take the train from Madrid down to the Royal Palace and garden at Aranjuez. The name of this small Spanish town is now world famous because of the wonderful Concierto de Aranjuez for guitar and orchestra composed by Joaquin Rodrigo Vidre, known as the first Marquis de Aranjuez. The piece is deservedly famous. It was composed by Rodrigo in 1939 and is thought to hark back to the stately, languid life of the 18th century in the huge Royal Palace. His widow, the Turkish pianist Victoria Kamhi, said the composition was in part a reaction to the loss of one of their children. I have also heard it said that it originated from his habit of going to the extensive royal gardens at Aranjuez to seek peace in troubled times. I am not sure this can be true since he didn`t spend much time in Spain between 1924 and 1939. Rodrigo became blind at an early age as a result of a bout of diphtheria, but this did not prevent his achieving a glittering career as composer and virtuoso pianist. Having said that, he and his wife did suffer times of great poverty and hardship. However, the almost instant success of the concerto brought lasting prosperity. The beauty of the music evokes the colour, drama and warmth that make Spain such an irresistible country for many, like myself, who have had the privilege of getting to know it in part.

I went to Atocha station and was a little bewildered since it is huge. I asked a railway employee for directions, but I`m afraid her answer sounded more like machine-gun fire than any language I could follow. My Spanish is reasonable if the speaker makes some allowance for the fact that I`m foreign. However, this young lady made no concessions. I got more helpful guidance at one of the newspaper stalls and headed for my train. I did not realise that I was about to get an eerie reminder of my early life in Glasgow. As a teenager, if I was coming home on the bus on a Friday night I could be almost certain that I would be joined by a talkative drunk. I would usually be told what a wonderful wife he had, why rangers or Celtic football club was the best team that could ever exist and how he would go back to his shipyard job if his leg wasn`t so badly injured, a leg that had coped quite well with leaping onto a moving bus in a state of inebriation. I rarely

94

thought of such encounters any more. However, I had no sooner taken my seat on the train to Aranjuez, a word that filled my mind with romantic glamour and a kinder world, than I was aware of someone sitting beside me who had obviously enjoyed a beverage before getting on. I was pleased to note that the trip only took about half an hour. I was less pleased when my new companion began to make noises of a "trying to attract your attention" type. He then rattled out a slurred line of Spanish words which contained the phrase "train to Aranjuez". I assumed he was asking me if this was the train for Aranjuez. I replied "si". I was then aware of him looking at me. I tried to pay no attention, but without seeing him I knew the look. I had seen it in the eyes of Glasgow drunks. I assume it resembles the look of great astronomers when a new planet swims into their ken or like biologists who come across a life form they have never seen before. I tried to ignore him but he continued to look. Eventually he said "que?". I told him I didn't understand. He repeated the rather vague question. I repeated the precise answer. He then said "Aranjuez" and I said "si". I noticed some of the other passengers beginning to follow this intriguing exchange with amusement. My companion then fell silent for a bit and then poured out a string of information. I made out the word "mujer" and knew for sure that he was the spiritual cousin of my former Glasgow bus companions. He was talking about his wife. I felt I now had a deeper understanding with the gentleman than any knowledge of Spanish could possible impart. It was so deep that I contemplated getting off at the next stop and waiting for a later train. I could almost feel myself counting to four and, sure enough, on cue he began to sing. I felt his interest in Aranjuez was probably not, like mine, prompted by a love of music, since he was clearly tone deaf, or worse, a graduate of the same school of musical torment that had tutored the Glasgow drunks who somehow, inexplicably, always mutilated Burns` beautiful song, "Annie Laurie". After this, no doubt moved by the pathos of his own performance, he lurched out of his seat and headed down the train. I hoped never to see him again. He has appeared in the occasional nightmare but not otherwise. That is the only encounter I have ever had with a drunken Spaniard.

It was with some excitement that I left the train at Aranjuez. There was a sign to the Royal Palace and gardens. I set off along what turned out to be a long, dusty track. At the end of it was an enormous, sombre looking residence. Beside it was the entrance to the garden. I went into the palace. It is made of brick and white stone and has baroque rooms, a hall of mirrors and a smoking room. It was still quite early in the year and the day was overcast. Perhaps that explains why I found the palace bleak and melancholy, as if it were nolstalgic for those great occasions of the past evoked by Rodrigo`s music. I went out to the gardens. Again, perhaps it was too early in the year, but I saw no colour. There were trees and bushes and pathways and the Tagus river flows past it. Nothing was speaking to me of the warmth and sensual beauty of the concerto. A few other people were strolling about, none giving any obvious sign of being overwhelmed. I left early, more impressed than before by the creative power of great art. It is quite probable that Aranjuez is much more beguiling later in the year. It is possible that I had already had a surfeit of great experiences. My only remaining hope was that the drunk would not be taking the train back to Madrid.

I liked the Spanish capital very much. I have only made one brief return visit but my impression was confirmed. I hope to return again soon and get to know it better.

Made in the USA
Middletown, DE
26 November 2018